COLLINS
PHRASE BOOKS

PORTUGUESE

Collins Phrase Books

FRENCH
GERMAN
ITALIAN
PORTUGUESE
SPANISH
SCANDINAVIAN
RUSSIAN
GREEK
YUGOSLAV
DUTCH
LATIN AMERICAN SPANISH

COLLINS
PHRASE BOOKS

PORTUGUESE

Compiled by
N. J. LAMB

COLLINS
LONDON AND GLASGOW

GENERAL EDITOR: J. B. FOREMAN, M.A.

First published 1969
Latest reprint 1972

CONTENTS

ÍNDICE DE MATÉRIAS

INTRODUCTION

General Information

This can be obtained from the Casa de Portugal, 20 Lower Regent Street, London, S.W.1. In Portugal the tourist can get information from the Commissariado do Turismo, Palácio Foz, Praça dos Restauradores, Lisbon; and there are tourist information centres in all the main towns.

Citizens of the United Kingdom and the Republic of Ireland do not require a visa for entering Portugal, provided their stay does not exceed 60 days. Valid passports are, of course, essential. The addresses of some Portuguese Consulates are:

47 Wilton Crescent, London, S.W.1.
1 Falkner Square, Liverpool, 8.
178 Cathedral Road, Cardiff, CF1 JG
200 St. Vincent Street, Glasgow, C.2.

Routes to Portugal

The usual route by rail is via London-Paris-Hendaye-Irun-Salamanca-Vilar Formoso-Lisbon. The sea voyage to Lisbon, which often affords the opportunity of spending some hours ashore at Corunna, Vigo, or Leixões (for Oporto), takes about three days. The usual sailings are from Southampton or London. In Lisbon the offices of most of the shipping companies are near the Cais do Sodré station. BEA and TAP (Transportes Aéreos Portugueses) have regular flights to Lisbon. The AA and RAC provide detailed information about motoring routes and requirements. In Portugal the principal office of the "Automóvel Clube de Portugal" is at 24 Rua Rosa Araújo, Lisbon, and the club has branches in Oporto and Coimbra.

Currency

Travellers from the United Kingdom must comply with British regulations concerning the foreign currency allowance. Travellers' cheques are cashed without difficulty in Portugal on presentation of the passport; the banks there require the traveller's address in Portugal.

The unit of currency is the "escudo", and the rate of exchange
1968 is approximately 70 escudos to the £. One escudo may be taken
equivalent to 3½d. There are 100 "centavos" in one escudo. A "cont
is 1,000 escudos.

Prices are written thus:

5 $40 (i.e. 5 escudos, 40 centavos)
$80 (i.e. 80 centavos)

Transport
Information at the travel agencies and railway stations. Expresses a
known as "Rápidos"; the "Comboio-Correio" is a stopping trai
Lisbon and Oporto have good tram and bus services at very reasonab
prices. Taxis are numerous.

Meals
Breakfast consists of coffee (or tea, if asked for) with rolls and butte
and, sometimes, jam. Luncheon is served as a rule between 12.30 an
2.00 p.m., dinner from 7.30 until about 9.00 p.m.; these times may var
but dinner is rarely served as late as in Spain. Afternoon tea is no
generally served unless specially requested; the tea is weak and perhap
not very satisfactory by British standards, but Portuguese cakes ai
good.

The café is very popular in Portugal, as in Spain. A small cup o
glass of coffee costs about 1 escudo, 50 centavos.

Tipping
In hotels and boarding houses a service charge of 10% is added to th
bill. But this need not exclude an extra tip if the tourist feels he has ha
good service from the employees. Taxi-drivers might receive a tip of 1
to 15% of the fare. Cloakroom tips vary from 1 $00 to 2 $50. Porter
have fixed charges, but a tip of perhaps 2 $50 could be given. Shoe
blacks might be given a small tip.

Entertainments
Cinemas show many American and British films. The sound-track i
not usually "dubbed"; only the sub-titles are in Portuguese. Ther
are night clubs in Lisbon and Oporto, but many visitors make for the
"Restaurantes Típicos" to hear the *fados*. Bull-fighting, from May to
October, is not so prominent as in Spain, nor, incidentally, is the bul
killed; football is much more popular. Facilities for tennis, golf, fishing
and camping are available: information on these and on the regional
fairs and festivals can be obtained from the tourist offices.

General

Attention should be paid to regulations concerning dress on beaches and when entering churches. On entering churches women should cover their heads and arms, and men should not enter in shorts.

To call a person's attention, for example in order to ask the way, or for service in a shop, one would preface one's request with "fazia favor" or "faz favor".

To call for attention in a café—though this is rarely necessary, since Portuguese waiters are alert—one can say "faz favor"; in cafés, some Portuguese are adept at hissing (*psst*!) for attention, but this is undignified and difficult for the foreigner to do well. It is not customary to clap one's hands or call out "criado" (waiter).

In the larger towns English is now understood and spoken by an increasing number of Portuguese. French is also widely known, and Spanish is, of course, readily understood.

PRONUNCIATION OF PORTUGUESE

The pronunciation of Portuguese is undoubtedly difficult,—much more so than Spanish. Hence, while a tourist knowing Spanish will have little difficulty in reading Portuguese and being understood when he speaks Spanish—or even when he attempts to speak Portuguese with a Spanish accent—, he will find it far from easy to understand what is being said to him in reply.

No transcription into English symbols can represent with complete accuracy the complexities of Portuguese sounds, a full description of which is beyond the limits of this book. A single letter may have different sounds, depending on its position in a word and on its relation to other letters: thus, *o* has three sounds, *s* has four. The pronunciation scheme used here, which is similar to that of *Collins' Portuguese Gem Dictionary*, can serve only as an approximation to the correct pronunciation. Portuguese is spoken with much "slurring" of unstressed syllables and linking together of words.

The stress in a word is usually on the last syllable but one (i.e. the penultimate). In the pronunciation scheme used here the stress is to be placed on the syllable immediately *preceding* the accent mark('): thus, in "quanto" (kwan'too) the stress is on the "an", in "lado" (lah'doo) on the "ah".

The spelling used throughout this book conforms to the rules of the *Acordo Luso-Brasileiro* of 1945.

Symbol employed	Portuguese spelling	Symbol represents approximately the following English sounds
ah	a	long open *a*, as in father, rather.
ar	ar	long open *a* plus trilled *r*, as in starry.
a	a	a somewhat shorter, but still open, *a*; like Northern English lad.
ă	a	close or "obscure" *a*, as in above, about, sofa.
ăr	ar	close *a* plus trilled *r*; approximately as in sugary, summary.
air	er	as in hairy, with trilled *r* always.
ay	e	as in stay, play, but without final glide.
ay-ee	ei	as in play, plus a rapidly spoken *ee*; roughly equivalent to the sharp cry hey!
e	e	as in bet, gem.
e-ee	éi	as in bet, plus rapidly spoken *ee*.
e-oo	éu	as in bet, plus rapidly spoken *oo*.
ě	e; i	close, "obscure" *e*, as in open, spoken.
ěr	er	close *e* as in open, plus trilled *r*; roughly as *er* in Everest, watery.
ee	i, e	as in meet, seen.
i	i, e	as in is, prince.
ish	es (when unstressed at beginning of word)	as in dish.
o	o	open *o*, as in top.
oh	o, ou	close *o*; a pure vowel as in Northern English cope, most.
or	or	as in for, organ, but with trilled *r*.
oh-ee	oi	as Northern English most, plus rapidly spoken *ee*; roughly as *owy* in showy.

Symbol employed	Portuguese spelling	Symbol represents approximately the following English sounds
oo	o, u	as in moon, too.
ow	au	as in now, how, cow.
oy	ói	as in boy.
ȳ	ai	as in style.
b	b	as in English.
d	d	as in English, but rather softer when between two vowels (though not as soft as in Spanish).
f	f	as in English.
g	g (+ consonant or a, o, u)	as in go, get.
k	c (+ consonant or a, o, u) / qu (+e, i)	as k in English.
ks	x, cç	as ks in books.
l	l	as in English.
ly	lh	as li in million.
m	m	as in English.
n	n	as in English.
ny	nh	as ny in canyon.
p	p	as in English.
r	r, rr	a strongly trilled r as in Scottish speech.
s	s, ss, x, ç, c (+ e, i)	as s in sun, house.
sh	s, ch, x, z	as in shop.
t	t	as in English.
v	v	as in English.
w	u, o	as w in win.
gw	go, gu (+ a)	as gw in wigwam.
kw	qu (+ a)	as kw in bookworm.
mw	mu (+ i)	as mw in tramway.
y	i (or part of sounds of "nh" and "lh")	as y in you.
z	s, z, x	as in English.
zh	s, z, j, g (+ e, i)	as s in measure.

Note: Portuguese *h* is always silent. *E* at the end of a word of more than one syllable is usually silent but is often sounded when the following word begins with a vowel. *E* meaning "and" is always pronounced *ee*. Final *s* followed by a word beginning with a vowel has the sound of English *z*.

Nasal Sounds

The nasalisation (i.e. pronouncing through the nose) of vowels and diphthongs is a notable feature of Portuguese pronunciation, though the intensity of the nasalisation is weaker than in French. Nasalisation is shown in the pronunciation scheme here by putting *n* after the vowel. For example, 'ee*n*' represents a nasalised 'ee' (the Portuguese word *sim* is pronounced "see*n*"), and "ow*n*" is the nasalised "ow" of English "how, now, cow" (thus Portuguese *não* is pronounced "now*n*").

Nasalisation is shown in Portuguese spelling either by inserting a "til" (˜) over a vowel, or by an 'm' at the end of a word (as in *bom, bem, aprendem*), or by 'm' or 'n' before a consonant (as in *quanto, comprar*).

BRAZILIAN PORTUGUESE

The Portuguese spoken in Brazil differs in some respects from that of Portugal, as American English differs from our own.

Generally, Brazilian pronunciation seems slower, more measured, with less linking of words, and is perhaps clearer to the English ear than the pronunciation of Portugal. The unstressed vowels, rapidly slurred over in Portugal, are heard more clearly in Brazil. Final *e* is sounded more frequently (e.g. "cidade": see-dah'dee), but sometimes palatalises the preceding consonant (e.g. "diferente": dee-fĕ-re*n*tsh'). *S* at the end of a syllable often remains as a "hard" *s* or *z*, instead of sounding as *sh* or *zh* (e.g. país: pa-ees'; escrevo: is-kray'voo; desde: dayz'dee).

In vocabulary also there are differences. For example: bonde=tramcar; cardápio=menu; discar=to dial a number; parada=bus stop; senhorita=young lady, Miss; terno=suit; trem=train.

SOME GRAMMATICAL NOTES
(*masc.*=masculine; *fem.*=feminine)

Nouns

All nouns in Portuguese are either masculine or feminine. Nouns ending in —o (except -ção, -são, -dão) are almost always masculine; those ending in —a, —ção, —são, —dade are almost always feminine. Nouns ending in —e or a consonant may be masculine or feminine.

The plural of nouns is formed by adding —s or, after most conson-

nts, —es: carro - carros; porta - portas; chave - chaves; mulher -
ulheres; mês - meses; luz - luzes.

Nouns ending in —ão generally change to —ões (pronounced
-oy*n*sh) in the plural; but note an exception: mão - mãos (hands).

Nouns ending in —l drop this —l and replace it usually by —is:
ornal - jornais.

Nouns ending in —m drop the —m and replace it by —ns: homem -
omens.

Definite Article (the)

	Singular	*Plural*		
Masc.	o (oo)	os (oosh)	o castelo	os castelos
Fem.	a (ă)	as (ăsh)	a carta	as cartas

Indefinite Article (a, an)

Masc.	um (oo*n*)	um castelo
Fem.	uma (oo'mă)	uma carta

N.B. In the vocabularies placed at the beginning of the various sections
of this book the insertion of *o* or *um, a* or *uma* before a noun indicates
the gender.

Adjectives

Adjectives ending in —o change this to —a with a feminine noun:
>   um livro pequeno
>   uma casa pequena

Note: 'estou cansado' (I am tired) becomes 'estou cansada' when
spoken by a woman. Similarly, a woman says 'obrigada' (thank you),
not 'obrigado'.

An adjective of nationality ending in —s adds —a in the feminine:
>   um livro inglês
>   uma casa inglesa

(A man says 'sou inglês'; a woman says 'sou inglesa').

> The plural of adjectives is formed by adding —s or —es:
> pequeno - pequenos; grande - grandes; inglês - ingleses.
> But adjectives ending in —l drop the —l and replace it
> by —is (or —eis):
> espanhol - espanhóis
> fácil - fáceis.

Comparison

Use *mais* ('more') before the adjective:
>   fácil ('easy');   mais fácil ('easier');   o mais fácil ('easiest').

But a few comparatives are irregular:

bom (good)	melhor (better)	o melhor (best)
mau (bad)	pior (worse)	o pior (worst)
grande (big)	maior (bigger)	o maior (biggest)

Pronouns

I	= eu (ay′oo)		we	= nós (nosh)
he	= ele (ayl)		they (*masc.*)	= eles (aylsh)
she	= ela (e′lă)		they (*fem.*)	= elas (e′lăsh)
it	= ele, ela			

you (*masc.*) = o senhor (oo sĕ-nyohr′)
you (*fem.*) = a senhora (ă sĕ-nyoh′ră)

you (*masc. plural*) = os senhores (oosh sĕ-nyoh′rĕsh)
you (*fem. plural*) = as senhoras (ăsh sĕ-nyoh′răsh)

Forms of address are complicated in Portuguese.
You. There is no simple translation of the English "you" which can be used in all situations. The basic form is "o senhor", etc. But the best plan is usually to avoid "you" altogether and use only the verb-form (as in the majority of the phrases in this book).

A very polite form of "you" when addressing a man of good social standing is 'Vossa Excelência (vos-esh-sĕ-len′see-ă); a polite "you" when addressing a lady—one's hostess, for example, or the wife or mother of a new acquaintance—is 'minha senhora' (mee′nyă sĕ-nyoh′ră). A maid in a hotel is addressed as "menina" (mĕ-nee′nă).

for me	= para mim (mee*n*)	for us	= para nós (nosh)	
for him	= para ele			
for her	= para ela	for them	= para eles; (*fem.*)	
			para elas	
for you	=para o senhor	for you	= para os senhores	
	(*fem.* a senhora)		(*fem.* as senhoras)	

Possessives

These agree with the thing possessed and not with the possessor.

(o) meu (*fem.* (a) minha)	my; mine.
(o) seu (*fem.* (a) sua)	your; yours.
dele (after the noun)	his.
dela (after the noun)	her; hers.
(o) nosso (*fem.* (a) nossa)	our; ours.
deles (after the noun), delas (*fem.*)	their; theirs.

meu livro	=	my book
sua gabardina	=	your raincoat
livro dele	=	his book
nossa pensão	=	our boarding house

Verbs

The present tense will often serve for the future also: e.g. vou lá amanhã=I shall go there tomorrow, I'm going there tomorrow; telefono esta noite=I'll phone tonight.

Vou plus the infinitive can also express the future as in English: e.g. vou escrever uma carta=I shall write a letter, I am going to write a letter.

Verbs ending in —AR, like FALAR (to speak):

Present Tense	Past Tense
falo, I speak	falei, I spoke, have spoken
fala, he, she, speaks; you speak	falou, he, she, spoke, has spoken; you spoke, have spoken
falamos, we speak	falámos, we spoke, have spoken
falam, they speak; you speak	falaram, they spoke, have spoken; you spoke, have spoken

(The ending in —am is pronounced 'ow*n*,' and -ou is 'oh')

Verbs ending in —ER, like APRENDER (to learn)

aprendo	aprendi
aprende	aprendeu
aprendemos	aprendemos
aprendem	aprenderam

(The ending in —em is pronounced 'e*n*', and -eu is 'ay-oo')

Verbs ending in —IR, like PARTIR (to depart, leave)

parto	parti
parte	partiu
partimos	partimos
partem	partiram

(The ending in —em is pronounced 'e*n*', and —iu is 'ee-oo')

There are two verbs meaning 'to be': SER and ESTAR. ESTAR is used for a temporary situation or condition, e.g. estou no hotel=I am in the hotel; o prato está na mesa=the plate is on the table; a sopa está fria=the soup is cold.

SER

sou, I am	fui, I was
é, he, she, it, is; you are	foi, he, she, it, was; you were
somos, we are	fomos, we were
são, they, you, are	foram, they, you, were

(são is pronounced 'sow*n*')

ESTAR

estou	estive
está	esteve
estamos	estivemos
estão	estiveram

(estão is pronounced 'ish-tow*n*')

Among the irregular verbs are the following:

TER (to have, possess)

tenho	tive
tem	teve
temos	tivemos
têm	tiveram

IR (to go)

vou	fui
vai	foi
vamos	fomos
vão	foram

VIR (to come)

venho	vim
vem	veio
vimos	viemos
vêm	vieram

DIZER (to say, tell)

digo	disse
diz	disse
dizemos	dissemos
dizem	disseram

FAZER (to do, make)

faço	fiz
faz	fez
fazemos	fizemos
fazem	fizeram

PODER (to be able)

posso	pude
pode	pôde
podemos	pudemos
podem	puderam

DAR (to give)

dou	dei
dá	deu
damos	demos
dão	deram

VER (to see)

vejo	vi
vê	viu
vemos	vimos
vêem	viram

Negatives

put *não* before the verb

tenho	=	I have
não tenho	=	I haven't
falo	=	I speak
não falo	=	I don't speak

Questions

Simple questions are generally asked by raising the pitch of the voice towards the end of the sentence:

o senhor vai? = are you going?

(o senhor vai = you are going)

SOME COMMON WORDS AND PHRASES

VOCABULARY

how, como (koh'moo)
how much, quanto (kwan'too), quanta (kwan'tă)
how many, quantos (kwan'toosh), quantas (kwan'tăsh)
this (one), este (aysh'tă)
that (one), aquele (ă-kayl')
when, quando (kwan'doo)
where, onde (ond)
why, porque (poor'kĕ); porquê? (poor-kay')
yes, sim (seen)
no, não (nown)

all, todo (toh'doo), toda (toh'dă), todos (toh'doosh),todas (toh'd ăsh)
almost, quase (kwah'zĕ)
also, as well, também (tan-ben')
enough, bastante (băsh-tant')
everybody, todos (toh'doosh)
everything, tudo (too'doo)
less, menos (may'noosh)
a little, um pouco (oon poh'koo)
much, a lot, muito (mween'too)
many, muitos (mween'toosh), muitas (mween'tăsh)
more, mais (mŷsh)
too many, muitos (mween'toosh)
too much, demais (dĕ-mŷsh')

very, muito (mween'too)
above, por cima (poor see'mă)
across, através de (ă-tră-vezh' dĕ)
after, depois (de) (dĕ-poh'eesh (dĕ))
against, contra (kon'tră)
among, entre (en'trĕ)
at, em (en), a (ă)
before, antes (de) (antsh (dĕ))
behind, detrás (de) (dĕ-trazh' (dĕ))
below, debaixo de (dĕ-bỹ'shoo dĕ), em baixo (en bỹ'shoo
beside, ao lado de (ow lah'doo dĕ)
between, entre (en'trĕ)
down, para baixo (pă'ră bỹ'shoo)
downstairs, em baixo (en bỹ'shoo)
everywhere, em toda a parte (en toh'da part)
except, salvo (sal'voo), excepto (eesh-se'too)
far, longe (lonzh)
for, para (pă'ră); por (poor)

22

in front of, diante de (dee-ant' dĕ)
here, aqui (ă-kee')
in, into, em (en)
inside, dentro (de) (den'troo (dĕ))
left, esquerdo (ish-kayr'doo), esquerda (ish-kayr'dă)
near, perto (de) (pair'too (dĕ))
on, sobre (soh'brĕ)
outside, fora (fo'ră)
over, sobre (soh'brĕ), por cima de (poor see'mă dĕ)
right, direito (dee-ray'ee-too), direita (dee-ray'ee-tă)
there, lá (lah), ali (ă-lee')
through, por (poor), através de (ă-tră-vezh' dĕ)
to, a (ă), para (pă'ră)
under, sob (sob)
until, até (ă-te')
upstairs, lá em cima (lah en see'mă)
with, com (kon)
without, sem (sen)

POLITE EXPRESSIONS

Please.	Faz favor; fazia favor; por favor.
	fash fă-vohr'; fă-zee'ă fă-vohr'; poor fă-vohr'
Thank you.	Obrigado; (*fem.*) obrigada.
	oh-bree-gah'doo; oh-bree-gah'dă
Thank you very much.	Muito obrigado.
	mween-to-bree-gah'doo
No, thank you.	(Não,) obrigado.
	(nown,) oh-bree-gah'doo
Good morning. Good afternoon. Good evening (night).	Bom dia. Boa tarde. Boa noite.
	bon dee'ă; boh'ă tard; boh'ă noh'eet
Good-bye.	Adeus.
	ă-day'oosh
Good-bye (*but meeting again soon*).	Até à vista; até logo.
	ă-te' ah veesh'tă; ă-te' lo'goo
Yes. No.	Sim. Não.
	seen; nown
Excuse me (I am sorry).	Desculpe; perdão.
	dish-koolp'; pĕr-down'

Excuse me (may I pass? may I come in? etc.)　　Com licença. Dá-me licença ?
kon lee-sen'să; da'mĕ lee-sen'-să

Excuse me (*to call a person's attention*).　　Faz favor.
fash fă-vohr'

Don't mention it; not at all.　　De nada; não tem de quê.
dĕ nah'dă; nown ten dĕ kay

Please sit down.　　Faz favor de sentar-se.
fash fă-vohr' dĕ sen-tar'sĕ

I am sorry (*forgive me*).　　Desculpe.
dish-koolp'

Please take my seat.　　Faz favor, sente-se aqui.
fash fă-vohr', sent'sĕ ă-kee'

How are you? Very well, thank you,—and you?　　Como está? Bem, obrigado, — e o senhor?
koh'moo ish-ta'; ben, o-bree-gah'doo,—ee oo sĕ-'nyohr'

May I introduce . . . ?　　Dá-me licença que lhe apresent
. . . .
da'mĕ lee-sensă kĕ lyĕ ă-prĕ-zent'

How do you do? (*on being introduced*).　　Muito prazer.
mween'too pră-zayr'

Am I disturbing you?—Not at all.　　Estou a incomodá-lo?—De modo nenhum.
ish-toh' ă een-koo-moo-da'loo; dĕ mo'doo nĕ-nyoon'

Please don't go to any trouble.　　Não se incomode, por favor.
nown sĕ een-koo-mod', poor fă-vohr'

Congratulations!　　Parabéns!
pă-ră-bensh'

Your health! (*in drinking toast*).　　(À sua) saúde!
(ah soo'ă) să-ood'

GENERAL DIFFICULTIES

I don't understand.　　Não percebo.
nown pĕr-say'boo

Do you speak English?   Fala inglês?
fa'lă een-glaysh'

Is there anyone here who speaks English?   Há aqui alguém que fale inglês?
ah ă-kee' al-gen' kĕ fal een-glaysh'

Can you speak French (Spanish, Italian)?   Fala francês (espanhol, italiano)?
fa'lă fran-saysh' (ish-pă-nyol', ee-tă-lee-ă'noo)

Can you translate (this) for me, please?   Pode traduzir (isto) para mim, por favor?
pod tră-doo-zeer (eesh'too) pă'ră meen, poor fă-vohr'

I don't understand Portuguese.   Não compreendo português.
nown kon-pree-en'doo poor-too-gaysh'

What is this in Portuguese?   Como se chama isto em português?
koh'moo sĕ shă'mă eesh'too en poor-too-gaysh'

How do you say . . . in Portuguese?   Como se diz . . . em português?
koh'moo sĕ deesh . . . en poor-too-gaysh'

I can't speak Portuguese.   Não falo português.
nown fa'loo poor-too-gaysh'

It is a difficult language.   É uma língua difícil.
e oo'mă leen'gwă dee-fee'seel

It is not easy.   Não é fácil.
nown e fah'seel

I understand, if you speak slowly.   Se falar devagar, percebo.
sĕ fă-lar' dĕ-vă-gar', pĕr-say'boo

Please speak slowly.   Faz favor de falar devagar.
fash fă-vohr' dĕ fă-lar' dĕ-vă-gar'

Please write it down.   Faz favor de o escrever.
fash fă-vohr' dee oo ish-krĕ-vayr'

Please repeat.   Diga outra vez, se faz favor.
dee'gă oh'tră vaysh, sĕ fash fă-vohr'

Wait, I am looking for the word (the phrase) in this book.   Espere, procuro a palavra (a frase) neste livro.
ish-pair', proo-koo'roo ă pă-lav'ră (ă frahz) naysht leev'roo

I am a foreigner.   Sou estrangeiro.
sou ish-tran-zhay'ee-roo

I am English (British), an American.
Sou inglês (*fem.* inglesa), americano (*fem.* americana
soh een-glaysh' (een-glay'ză), ă-mĕ-ree-kă'noo ('lă), ă-mĕ-ree-kă'nă)

Can I help you?
Posso ajudá-lo (-la *fem.*)?
po'soo ă-zhoo-da'loo ('lă)

Can you help me?
Pode ajudar-me?
pod ă-zhoo-dar'mĕ

Can you help me? (*e.g.* with information)
Pode dar-me uma informação
pod dar'mee oo'mă een-foor-mă-sown'

Do you need something?
Precisa de alguma coisa?
prĕ-see'ză dal-goo'mă koh'ee-ză

I have lost ...
Perdi ...
pĕr-dee'

I have already paid.
Já paguei.
zhah pă-gay'ee

Help!
Socorro!
soo-koh'roo

Call the police!
Chame a polícia!
sham ă poo-lee'see-ă

Come quickly!
Venha depressa!
ve'nyă dĕ-pre'să

Wait!
Espere!
ish-pair'

Fire!
Fogo!
foh'goo

Thief!
Ladrão!
lă-drown'

Where are we going?
Aonde vamos?
ă-ond' vă'moosh

Where are you going?
Para onde vai?
pă'ră ond vỹ

I am looking for ...
Procuro ...
proo-koo'roo

What do you want?
Que quer?
kĕ kair

That man is following me everywhere.
Aquele homem segue-me por toda a parte.
ă-kayl' o'men seg'mĕ poor toh'da part

shall call a policeman. Vou chamar um polícia.
voh shă-mar' oon poo-lee'see-ă

et a policeman. Chame um guarda.
sham oon gwar'dă

'ho are you? Quem é o senhor (*fem.* a senhora)?
ken e oo sĕ-nyohr' (ă sĕ-nyoh'ră)

don't know you. Não o conheço.
nown oo koo-nyay'soo

don't know him (her). Não o (a) conheço.
nown oo (ă) koo-nyay'soo

don't want to speak to you. Não quero falar consigo.
nown kair'oo fă-lar' kon-see'goo

eave me alone! Go away! Deixe-me. Vá-se embora.
day'shĕ-mĕ. va'sen-bo-ră

'hat is the matter? O que é que se passa?
oo kee e kĕ sĕ pa'să

ou are mistaken. Enganou-se.
en-gă-noh'sĕ

'hat must I do? Que tenho que fazer?
kĕ te'nyoo kĕ fă-zayr'

did not know the rules. Não conhecia as regras.
nown koo-nyĕ-see'ă ăzh re'grăsh

'here is . . . ? Onde é . . . ?; (temporary position) Onde está . . . ?
on'dee e; ond ish-ta'

'here do I apply? Onde devo dirigir-me?
ond day'voo dee-ree-zheer'mĕ

'here do I go? Onde hei-de ir?
on'dee ay dĕ eer

'ly address is . . . ; I am staying at (the hotel . . .) A minha direcção é . . . ; estou no (hotel . . .)
ă mee'nyă dee-re-sown' e . . . ; ish-toh' noo (oh-tel' . . .)

MISCELLANEOUS EXPRESSIONS

s it ready? Are you ready? Está pronto?
ish-ta' pron'too

Bring . . .	Traga . . . trah′gă
Come here.	Venha cá. ve′nyă ka
Come with me.	Venha comigo. ve′nyă koo-mee′goo
Come in.	Entre. en′trĕ
You can go.	Pode ir. pod eer
Don't do that.	Não faça isso. nown fah′să ee′soo
Don't forget.	Não se esqueça. nown see ish-ke′să
Listen! Look!	Ouça! Olhe! oh′să. o′lyĕ
Will it be long?	Demora muito? dĕ-mo′ră mween′too
Look out!	Cuidado! Atenção! kwee-dah′doo. ă-ten-sown′
Nothing else?	Mais nada? mÿzh nah′dă
That's enough. That will do.	Basta. Chega. bash′tă. she′gă
Finished.	Acabado. ă-kă-bah′doo
I am hungry, thirsty.	Tenho fome, sede. te′nyoo fom, sayd
I am hot, cold.	Tenho calor, frio. te′nyoo kă-lohr′, free′oo
I am tired.	Estou cansado. ish-toh′ kan-sah′doo
I am in a hurry.	Estou com pressa. ish-toh′ kon pre′să
As soon (early) as possible.	O mais cedo possível. oo mÿsh say′doo poo-see′vel
Take it easy! Calm down!	Calma! kal′mă

Slowly.	Devagar.
	dĕ-vă-gar'
Quickly.	Depressa.
	dĕ-pre'să
I don't know.	Não sei.
	nown say'ee
I think so.	Julgo que sim.
	zhool'goo kĕ seen
Don't you think so?	Não acha?
	nown ah'shă
Isn't it, etc. (cf. French *n'est-ce pas*).	Não é (verdade)?
	nown e vĕrdad'
What a pity!	Que pena!
	kĕ pay'nă
It's not worth while.	Não vale a pena.
	nown val ă pay'nă
I want . . . ; I should like . . .	Quero . . . ; Queria . . ?
	kair'oo . . . ; kĕ-ree'ă . . .
I like . . .	Gosto de . . .
	gosh'too dĕ . . .
Who is it? Who is there?	Quem é?
	ken e
Where can we have something to eat?	Onde podemos comer?
	ond poo-day'moosh koo-mayr'
Where can I wash my hands?	Onde posso lavar as mãos?
	ond po'soo lă-var' ăzh mownsh
Where is the lavatory?	Onde é a toilette, o lavatório, a casa de banho?
	on'dee e ă twa-let', oo lă-vă-to'ree-oo, ă kah'ză dĕ bă'nyoo
Where is the Post Office?	Onde é o correio?
	on'dee e oo koo-ray'yoo
Where is the Police Station?	Onde é a esquadra da Polícia?
	on'dee e ă ish-kwa'dră dă poo-lee'see-ă
Where is the British Consulate?	Onde é o consulado britânico?
	on'dee e oo kon-soo-lah'doo bree-tă'nee-koo

Where is the hotel (boarding house? Onde é o hotel (a pensão)?

on'dee e oo oh-tel' (ă pen-sown')

Where is the station? Onde é a estação?

on'dee e ă ish-tă-sown'

TIME

VOCABULARY

morning, a manhã (mă-nyan')
afternoon, a tarde (tard)
evening, a tarde (tard); (after dark) a noite (noh'eet)
night, a noite (noh'eet)
today, hoje (ohzh)
tomorrow, amanhã (a-mă-nyan')
yesterday, ontem (on'ten)
tonight, esta noite (esh'tă noh'eet)

after, depois (dĕ-poh'eesh)
always, sempre (sen'prĕ)
at once, imediatamente; já (ee-mĕ-dee-ĕ-tă-ment'; zhah)
beginning, o começo (koo-may'soo)
calendar, o calendário (kă-len-dah'ree-oo)
clock, o relógio (rĕ-lo'zhee-oo)
day, o dia (dee'ă)
during, durante (doo-rant')
early, cedo (say'doo)
end, o fim (feen)
first, (o) primeiro (pree-may'ee-roo)
hour, a hora (o'ră)
last, (o) último (ool'tee-moo)
late, tarde (tard)
later, mais tarde (mÿsh tard), logo (lo'goo)
middle, o meio (may'yoo)
never, nunca (noon'kă)
next, próximo (pro'see-moo)
now, agora (ă-go'ră)
often, muitas vezes (mween'tăsh vay'zĕsh), frequentemente (frĕ-kwen-tĕ-ment')
presently, já (zhah)
sometimes, algumas vezes (al-goo'măzh vay'zĕsh)
shortly, em breve (en brev)
since, desde (dayzh'dĕ)
soon, cedo (say'doo); em breve (en brev)
then, depois (dĕ-poh'eesh)

time, a hora (o'răr); (in general sense) o tempo (ten'poo)
watch, o relógio (rĕ-lo'zhee-oo)
week, uma semana (sĕ-mä'nă); oitn dias (oh'ee-too dee'-ăsh)

What time is it?   Que horas são?
kee o'răsh sown

It is one o'clock.   É uma hora.
e oo'mă o'ră

It is two, three, four o'clock, etc.   São duas horas, três horas, quatro horas, etc.
sown doo'ăz o'răsh, trayz o'răsh, kwa'troo o'răsh . . .

At one o'clock.   À uma hora.
ah oo'mă o'ră

At two o'clock, at three, etc.   Às duas, às três, etc.
azh doo'ăzh, ash trayzh . . .

It is twelve o'clock (midday).   É meio-dia.
e may'yoo dee'ă

It is twelve o'clock (midnight).   É meia-noite.
e may'yă noh'eet

It is half past twelve (12.30 p.m.)   É meio-dia e meia (hora).
e may'yoo dee'ă ee may'yă (o'ră)

It is half past twelve (12.30 a.m.)   É meia-noite e meia (hora).
e may'yă noh'eet ee may'yă (o'ră)

At nine o'clock in the morning.   Às nove (horas) da manhã.
azh nov (o'răsh) dă mă-nyan'

It is five past one.   É uma hora e cinco.
e oo'mă o'ră ee seen'koo

It is a quarter past one.   É uma hora e um quarto.
e oo'mă o'ră ee oon kwar'too

It is half past one.   É uma hora e meia.
e oo'mă o'ră ee may'yă

It is a quarter to one.   É uma menos um quarto.
e oo'mă may'nooz oon kwar'too

It is ten past two.   São duas horas e dez.
sown doo'ăz o'răz ee desh

It is half past five.   São cinco (horas) e meia.
sown seen'koo (o'răz) ee may'ya

It is twenty to nine.	São vinte para as nove.
	(São nove menos vinte).
	sow*n* vee*nt* pă'razh nov (sow*n* nov may'noozh vee*nt*)
It is a quarter to seven.	São sete menos um quarto.
	sow*n* set may'nooz oon kwar'too
It is early.	É cedo.
	e say'doo
It is late.	É tarde.
	e tard
I want to get up early.	Quero levantar-me cedo.
	kai'roo lĕ-va*n*-tar'mĕ say'doo
Can you call me early in the morning?	Pode chamar-me de manhã cedo?
	pod shă-mar'mĕ dĕ mă-nyan' say'doo
This morning.	Esta manhã.
	esh'tă mă'nyan'
This afternoon.	Esta tarde.
	esh'tă tard
This evening.	Esta noite.
	esh'tă noh'eet
Tomorrow morning.	Amanhã de manhã.
	ah-mă-nyan' dĕ mă-nyan'
Tomorrow afternoon.	Amanhã à tarde.
	ah-mă-nyan' ah tard
Yesterday morning.	Ontem de manhã.
	on'te*n* dĕ mă-nyan'
Yesterday afternoon.	Ontem à tarde.
	on'te*n* ah tard
Last night.	A noite passada.
	ă noh'eet pă-sah'dă
The day after tomorrow.	Depois de amanhã.
	dĕ-poh'eezh dah-mă-nyan'
The day before yesterday.	Anteontem.
	a*n*-tee-on'te*n*
All day.	Todo o dia.
	toh'doo dee'ă
Every day.	Todos os dias.
	toh'dooz oozh dee'ăsh

Next week.	A próxima semana.
	ă pro'see-mă sĕ-mă'nă
Last week.	A semana passada.
	ă sĕ-mă'nă pă-sah'dă
A week ago.	Há uma semana.
	ah oo'mă sĕ-mă'nă
A fortnight.	Quinze dias.
	keen'zĕ dee'ăsh
A fortnight from now.	De hoje a quinze dias.
	dee ohzh ă keen'zĕ dee'ăsh
In a fortnight.	Dentro de quinze dias.
	den'troo de keen'zĕ dee'ăsh
In a week's time.	De hoje a oito dias.
	dee ohzh ă oh'ee-too dee'ăsh
In four days' time (four days from now).	De hoje a quatro dias.
	dee ohzh ă kwa'troo dee'ăsh

DAYS OF THE WEEK

Sunday, domingo (doo-meen'goo)
Monday, segunda-feira (sĕ-goon'dă fay'ee-ră)
Tuesday, terça-feira (tayr'să fay'ee-ră)
Wednesday, quarta-feira (kwar'tă fay'ee-ră)
Thursday, quinta-feira (keen'tă fay'ee-ră)
Friday, sexta-feira (saysh'tă fay'ee-ră)
Saturday, sábado (sa'bă-doo)

In timetables and public notices the days from Monday to Friday are often abbreviated, e.g.: às 2as (*or, às segundas*): *on Mondays.*
às 6as (*or, às sextas*): *on Fridays.*

On Sunday.	No domingo.
	noo doo-meen'goo
Last Monday.	A segunda-feira passada.
	ă sĕ-goon'dă fay'ee-ră pă-sah'dă
Next Tuesday.	A próxima terça-feira.
	ă pro'see-mă tayr'să fay'ee-ră
Since Saturday.	Desde sábado.
	dayzh'dĕ sa'bă-doo

A holiday.	Um dia feriado.
	oon dee'ă fĕ-ree-ah'doo
A working day.	Um dia de trabalho.
	oon dee'ă dĕ tră-ba'lyoo
A week-day.	Um dia de semana.
	oon dee'ă dĕ sĕ-mă'nă
Holidays.	As férias.
	ăsh fe'ree-ăsh
Christmas.	O Natal.
	oo nă-tal'
New Year's Day.	O dia de Ano Novo.
	oo dee'ă dă'noo noh'voo
Easter.	A Páscoa.
	ă pash'kwă
Whitsuntide.	O Pentecostes.
	oo pen-tĕ-koshtsh'

(The following are national holidays in addition to the above).

Corpus Christi Day.	O dia do Corpo de Deus.
	oo dee'ă doo kohr'poo dĕ day'oosh
June 10th.	O dia de Camões; dia da Raça
	oo dee'ă dĕ kă'moynsh; dee'ă dă ra'să
August 15th.	O dia da Assunção.
	oo dee'ă da-soon-sown'
October 5th.	O dia da República.
	oo dee'ă dă re-poo'blee-kă
November 1st. (All Saints)	O dia de Todos os Santos.
	oo dee'ă dĕ toh'dooz oosh san'toosh
December 1st.	O Primeiro de Dezembro.
	oo pree-may'ee-roo dĕ dĕ-zen'broo
December 8th.	O dia da Imaculada Conceicão
	oo dee'ă dă ee-mă-koo-lah'dă kon-say-sown'

MONTHS AND SEASONS

January, janeiro (zhă-nay'ee-roo)
February, fevereiro (fĕ-vray'ee-roo)
March, março (mar'soo)

April, abril (ă-breel')
May, maio (mȳ'yoo)
June, junho (zhoo'nyoo)
July, julho (zhoo'lyoo)
August, agosto (ă-gohsh'too)
September, setembro (sĕ-ten'broo)
October, outubro (oh-too'broo)
November, novembro (noo-ven'broo)
December, dezembro (dĕ-zen'broo)

spring, a primavera (pree-mă-vair'ă)
summer, o verão (vĕ-rown')
autumn, o outono (oh-toh'noo)
winter, o inverno (een-vair'noo)
month, o mês (maysh)
months, os meses (may'zĕsh)
season, a estação [do ano] (ish-tă-sown' [doo ă'noo])
seasons, as estações (ish-tă-soynsh')

year, o ano (ă'noo)

n spring. In summer, etc.	Na primavera. No verão, etc.
	nă pree-mă-vair'ă; noo vĕ-rown'
une 1st.	O primeiro de junho.
	oo pree-may'ee-roo dĕ zhoo'nyoo
uly 4th.	O dia quatro de julho.
	oo dee'ă kwa'troo dĕ zhoo'lyoo
low long have you been here?	Há quanto tempo está cá?
	ah kwan'too ten'poo ish-ta' ka
have been here since Sunday.	Estou cá desde domingo.
	ish-toh' ka dayzh'dĕ doo-meen'goo
have been here four days.	Há quatro dias que estou cá.
	ah kwa'troo dee'ăsh kee ish-toh' ka
Ve have been here a week.	Há uma semana que estamos cá.
	ah oo'mă sĕ-mă'nă kee ish-tă'moosh ka
low long are you staying?	Quanto tempo vão passar aqui?
	kwan'too ten'poo vown pa-sar' ă-kee'
Ve shall stay here for (about) five days.	Vamos passar (uns) cinco dias aqui.
	vă'moosh pă-sar' (oonsh) seen'koo dee'ăsh ă-kee'
Vhen are you leaving?	Quando partem?
	kwan'doo par'ten

TRAVEL

PLANE

by air, by plane, đe avião (da-vee-own')
air hostess, a hospedeira đe borđo (ohsh-pĕ-day'ee-ră đĕ bor'đoo)
airline, a companhia aérea (kon-pă-nyee'ă ă-air'ee-a)
airport, o aeroporto (air-oh-pohr'too)
air-sickness, enjôo (en-zhoh'oo)
announcement, o aviso (ă-vee'zoo)
arrival, a chegada (shĕ-gah'đă)
cabin, a cabina (kă-bee'nă)
class, a classe (klas)
clouds, as nuvens (ăzh noo'vensh)
cotton-wool, o algodão em rama (all-goo-down en ră'mă)
crew, a tripulação (tree-poo-lă-sown')
departure, partida (păr-tee'đă)
emergency exit, saída de emergência (să-ee'đă dee-mĕr-zhen'see-ă)
flight, o vôo (voh'oo)
fly, to, voar (voo-ar')
fog, o nevoeiro (nĕ-voo-ay'ee-roo)
jet plane, o avião a jacto (ă-vee-own' ă zha'too)
land, a terra (te'ră)
land, to, aterrar (ă-tĕ-rar')
oxygen mask, a máscara de oxigénio (mash'kă-ră dok-see-zhe'nee-o
passenger, o passageiro (pă-să-zhay'ee-roo)
pilot, o piloto (pee-loh'too)
pilot's report, o relatório de vôo (rĕ-lă-to'ree-oo đĕ voh'oo)
plane, o avião (ă-vee-own')
propeller, a hélice (e'lees)
runway, a pista [de descolagem] (peesh'tă đĕ dish-koo-lah'zhen)
seat, o lugar (loo-gar')
seat belt, o cinto de segurança (seen'too đĕ sĕ-goo-ran'să)
steward, despenseiro (dish-pen-say'ee-roo)
take off, to, descolar (dish-koo-lar'), sair (să-eer')
ticket, o bilhete (bee-lyayt')
timetable, o horário (oo-rah'ree-oo)
toilet, a toilette (twa-let')
tourist, um turista (too-reesh'tă)
tourist class, a classe turística (klas too-reesh'tee-kă)
tray, a bandeja (ban-day'zhă)
window, a janela (zhă-ne'lă)
wing, a asa (ah'ză)

Where is the Airline Office?   Onde é a agência aérea?
　　　on'dee e a-zhen'see-ă ă-air'ee-ă

Where is the TAP, BOAC, etc.   Onde é a agência do TAP,
　　office?   BOAC, etc.?
　　　　on'dee e a-zhen'see-ă doo tap, bay-oh-ah-say . . .

I want to reserve a seat (two   Quero reservar um lugar (dois
　seats) in the plane for . . .   lugares) no avião para . . .
　kair'oo rě-zěr-var' oon loo-gar' (doh'eezh loo-gar'ěsh) noo ă-vee-own' pă'ră . . .

Is there a plane from here to . . .?   Há avião daqui para . . . ?
　　　　ah ă-vee-own' dă-kee' pă'ră . . .

What time does the plane leave?   A que horas parte o avião?
　　　ă kee o'răsh part oo ă-vee-own'

When do we reach . . . . ?   Quando chegamos a . . . ?
　　　　kwan'doo shě-gă'mooz ă . . .

Can I go direct?   Posso ir directamente?
　　　　po'soo eer dee-re-tă-ment'

Does the plane stop anywhere   O avião pára em algum sítio
　en route?   antes de chegar a . . . ?
　　　oo ă-vee-own' pah'ră en al'goon see'tee-oo antsh dě shě-gar' ă . . .

Can I break my flight at . . . ?   Posso interromper o vôo em
　　　　　　　　　　　　　　　　　. . . . ?
　　　po'soo een-tě-ron-payr' oo voh'oo en . . .

What is the fare (single, return)?   Quanto é a passagem (de ida, de
　　　　　　　　　　　　　　　　ida e volta)?
　　　kwan'too e ă pă-sah'zhen (dee'dă, dee'dă ee vol'tă)

How do I get to the airport?   Como se vai para o aeroporto?
　　　koh'moo sě vy pă'roo air-oh-pohr'too

Is there transport?   Há transporte?
　　　　　ah transh-port'

How much luggage can I take?   Quanta bagagem posso levar?
　　　kwan'tă bă-gah'zhen po'soo lě-var'

What is the charge?   Quanto custa?
　　　　kwan'too koosh'tă

What is the excess charge?   Quanto é o excesso?
　　　kwan'too e oo ish-se'soo

I have to cancel my reservation.   Tenho de cancelar a reserva de
　　　　　　　　　　　　　　　　lugar.
　　　te'nyoo dě kan-sě-lar' ă rě-zair'vă dě loo-gar'

Can I change my seat?	Posso mudar de lugar?
	po'soo moo-dar' dĕ loo-gar'
Put out your cigarettes and fasten your seat belts, please.	Por favor, apaguem os cigarre e apertem os cintos de segu ança.
	poor fǎvohr', ǎ-pa'gen oosh see-ga'roosh ee ǎ-pair'ten oosh seen'toosh dĕ sĕ-goo-ran'sǎ
We are about to take off.	Estamos prestes a levantar vôo.
	ish-tǎ'moosh preshts ǎ lĕ-van-tar' voh'oo
I cannot fasten my seat belt.	Não sou capaz de apertar meu cinto de segurança.
	nown soh kǎ-pazh' dee ǎ-pĕr-tar' oo may'oo seen'too dĕ sĕ-goo-ran'sǎ
Will you bring . . . please.	Faz favor de trazer . . .
	fash fǎ-vohr' dĕ trǎ-zayr' . . .
I don't feel well.	Não me sinto bem.
	nown mĕ seen'too ben
I feel sick.	Sinto-me enjoado (fem. enjoada).
	seen'too-mĕ en-zhoo-ah'doo (en-zhoo-ah'dǎ)

SHIP

by sea, de barco (dĕ bar'koo) [=in a ship]
alarm signal, o sinal de alarme (see-nal' da-larm')
baggage, a bagagem (bǎ-gah'zhen)
baggage room, a sala de bagagem (sa'lǎ dĕ bǎ-gah'zhen)
bar, o bar (bar)
berth, o beliche (bĕ-leesh')
cabin, o camarote (kǎ-mǎ-rot')
captain, o capitão (kǎ-pee-town')
crew, a tripulação (tree-poo-lǎ-so wn')
(member of the) crew um dos tripulantes (oon doosh tree-poo-lantsh
deck, a coberta (koo-bair'tǎ)
dining room, a sala de jantar (sa'lǎ dĕ zhan-tar')
dock, o cais (kỹsh)
fan, a ventoinha (ven-too-ee'nyǎ)
first class, a primeira classe (pree-may'ee-rǎ klas)
games, os jogos (zho'goosh)
gangway, o portaló (poor-tǎ-lo')
ladder, a escada (ish-kah'dǎ)
lifebelt, o cinto de salvação (seen'too de sal-vǎ-sown')

lifeboat, o barco salva-vidas (bar'koo sal'vă vee'dăsh)
lounge, o salão (să-lown')
luggage, a bagagem (bă-gah'zhen)
luggage room, a sala de bagagem (sa'lă dě bă-gah'zhen)
officer, o oficial (oo-fee-see-al')
playroom, a sala de jogos (sa'lă dě zho'goosh)
port, harbour, o porto (pohr'too)
porthole, a vigia (vee-zhee'ă)
purser, o comissário de bordo (koo-mee-sah'ree-oo dě bor'doo)
purser's office, o escritório (ish-kree-to'ree-oo)
raft, a jangada (zhan-gah'dă)
sailor, seaman, o marinheiro (mă-ree-nyay'ee-roo)
sea, o mar (mar)
ship, o navio (nă-vee'oo)
shipping agents, a agência de navegação (ă-zhen'see-ă dě nă-vě-gă-sown')
shipping line, a companhia de navegação (kon-pă-nyee'ă dě nă-vě-gă-sown')
(cabin) steward, o camaroteiro (kă-mă-roo-tay'ee-roo)
(chief) steward, o criado-chefe (kree-ah'doo shef)
stewardess, a criada de bordo (kree-ah'dă dě bor'doo)
swimming pool, a piscina (peesh-see'nă)
tourist class, a classe turística ((klas too-reesh'tee-kă)
ventilator, o ventilador (ven-tee-lă-dohr')
voyage, a viagem (vee-ah'zhen)

want to book a passage to ... Queria reservar passagem para
kě-ree'ă rě-zěr-var' pă-sah'zhen pă'ră ...

an I take my car with me? Posso levar o meu carro?
po'soo lě-var' oo may'oo ka'roo

hen is the sailing date (arrival Qual é a data da saída (da
date)? chegada)?
kwal e ă da'tă dă să-ee'dă (dă shě-gah'dă)

om which dock? De que cais?
dě kě kỹsh

hich is the way to the dock? Qual é o caminho para o cais?
kwal e oo kă-mee'nyoo pro kỹsh

hen do we embark? A que horas embarcamos?
ă kee o'răz en-băr-kă'moosh

hen do we sail? Quando partimos?
kwan'doo păr-tee'moosh

ll you show me my cabin? Pode indicar-me o meu camarote?
pod een-dee-kar'mee oo may'oo kă-mă-rot'

Can I change my berth?	Posso mudar de beliche? po'soo mood-ar' dĕ bĕ-leesh'
Which is the way on deck?	Por onde se vai à coberta? poor ond sĕ vȳ ah koo-bair'tă
Which is the way below?	Por onde se vai lá para baixo poor ond se vȳ lah pă'ră by'shoo
Where is the dining room?	Onde é a sala de jantar? ond'ee e ă sa'lă dĕ zhan-tar'
Where is the lounge, the bar?	Onde é o salão, o bar? ond'ee e oo să-lown', oo bar
Where is the purser's office?	Onde é o escritório? ond'ee e oo ish-kree-to'ree-oo
When does it open?	Quando abre? kwan'doo ab'rĕ
I want to change some money.	Quero cambiar dinheiro. kair'oo kan-bee-ar' dee-nyay'ee-roo
I can't find my luggage.	Não encontro a minha bagagem. nown en-kon'troo ă mee'nyă bă-gah'zhen
My luggage is not all here.	Não está aqui toda a minha bagagem. nown ish-ta' ă-kee' toh'da mee'nyă bă-gah'zhen
A case, a package, is missing.	Falta uma mala, um pacote. fal'tă oo'mă ma'lă, oon pă-kot'
Will you close the porthole?	Faz favor de fechar a vigia. fash fă-vohr' dĕ fĕ-shar' ă vi-zhee'ă
Is there a ventilator?	Há um ventilador? ah oon ven-tee-lă-dohr'
The fan does not work.	A ventoinha não funciona. ă ven-too-ee'nyă nown foon-see-oh'nă
I need another pillow, blanket.	Preciso de outra almofada, outro cobertor. prĕ-see'zoo doh'tră al-moo-fah'dă, oh'troo koo-bĕr-tohr'
I need a towel, soap.	Preciso de uma toalha, sabonete. prĕ-see'zoo doo'mă too-a'lyă, dĕ să-boo-nayt'
I need some drinking water.	Preciso de água para beber. prĕ-see'zoo dag'wă pă'ră bĕ-bayr'

feel sick.	Sinto-me enjoado.
	seen'too-mĕ en-zhoo-ah'doo
Bring a basin.	Traga uma bacia.
	trah'gă oo'mă bă-see'ă
Bring me a brandy.	Traga um brandy.
	trah'gă oon bran'dee
Bring me something to drink.	Traga-me qualquer coisa para beber.
	trah'gă-mĕ kwal'kair koh'ee-ză pă'ră bĕ-bayr'
feel better.	Sinto-me melhor.
	seen'too-mĕ mĕ-lyor'
hope you will feel better.	Estimo as suas melhoras.
	ish-tee'moo ăsh soo'ăzh mĕ-lyor'ăsh
want a deck-chair.	Quero uma cadeira de convés.
	kair'oo oo'mă kă-day'ee-ră dĕ kon-vesh'
What is the charge?	Quanto custa?
	kwan'too koosh'tă
When does the ship reach . . . ?	Quando chega o barco a . . . ?
	kwan'doo shay'gă oo bar'koo ă . . .
Can we go ashore in . . . ?	Podemos desembarcar em . . . ?
	poo-day'moozh dĕ-zen-băr-kar' en . . .
Must I get a landing-ticket?	Preciso de um cartão de desembarque?
	prĕ-see'zoo doon kăr-town' dĕ dĕ-zen-bark'
Do we need to take our passports?	É preciso levar os passaportes?
	e prĕ-see'zoo lĕ-var' oosh pa-să-portsh'
Are the passports examined on board?	Os passaportes são vistos a bordo?
	oosh pa-să-portsh' sown veesh'tooz ă bor'doo

TRAIN

VOCABULARY

arrival, a chegada (shĕ-gah'dă)
booking office, a bilheteira (bee-lyĕ-tay'ee-ră)
bookstall, o quiosque (kee-oshk')

coach, a carruagem (kǎ-roo-ah'zhen)
communication cord, o sinal de alarme (see-nal' da-larm')
compartment, o compartimento (kon-par-tee-men'too)
conductor, o revisor (rě-vee-zohr')
departure, a partida (pǎr-tee'dǎ)
dining car, o vagão-restaurante (vǎ-gown' rěsh-tow-rant')
door, a porta (por'tǎ)
driver, o maquinista (mǎ-kee-neesh'tǎ)
engine, a máquina (ma'kee-nǎ)
enquiry office, as informações (een-foor-mǎ-soynsh')
entrance, a entrada (en-trah'dǎ)
exit, a saída (sǎ-ee'dǎ)
gentlemen (lavatory), senhores (sě-nyoh'rěsh), homens (o'mensh)
guard, o guarda-freios (gwar'dǎ fray'yoosh)
journey, a viagem (vee-ah'zhen)
ladies (lavatory), senhoras (sě-nyohrǎsh)
left-luggage office, o depósito de bagagem (dě-po'zee-too dě bǎ-gah'zhen)
level-crossing, a passagem de nível (pǎ-sah'zhen dě nee'vel)
luggage van, o furgão (foor-gown')
non-smoking (compartment), proibido fumar (proo-ee-bee'doo foo-mar')
office, o escritório (ish-kree-to'ree-oo)
official, o funcionário (foon-see-oo-nah'ree-oo)
passenger, o passageiro (pǎ-sǎ-zhay'ee-roo)
platform, o cais (kỹsh), a linha (lee'nyǎ)
platform ticket, o bilhete de gare (bee-lyayt' dě gar)
porter, o bagageiro (bǎ-gǎ-zhay'ee-roo)
rack, a rede (rayd)
railway, o caminho de ferro (kǎ-mee'nyoo dě fe'roo)
rest (arm-), o descanso (dish-kan'soo)
seat, o assento (ǎ-sen'too), o lugar (loo-gar')
seat (reserved), um lugar reservado (loo-gar' rě-zěr-vah'doo)
station, a estação (ish-tǎ-sown')
stationmaster, o chefe de estação (shef dish-tǎ-sown')
telephone box, a cabine telefónica (kǎ-been' tě-lě-fon'ee-kǎ)
ticket, o bilhete (bee-lyayt')
ticket collector, o revisor (rě-vee-zohr')
time-table, o horário (oo-rah'ree-oo)
toilet, a toilette (twa-let'), o lavatório (lǎ-vǎ-to'ree-oo)
train, o comboio (kon-boy'oo)
tunnel, o túnel (too'nel)
waiting room, a sala de espera (sa'lǎ dish-pair'ǎ)
water (drinking), a água (potável) (a'gwǎ poo-tah'vel)
window, a janela (zhǎ-ne'lǎ)

Which is the way to the station, please? Faz favor, qual é o caminh para a estação?

fash fǎvohr', kwal e oo kǎ-mee'nyoo pǎ-rah' ish-tǎ-sown'

Where is the booking office?   Onde é a bilheteira?
on'dee e ă bee-lyĕ-tay'ee-ră

Where is the enquiry office?   Onde são as informações?
ond sown ăz een-foor-mă-soynsh'

Where is the time-table?   Onde está o horário?
ond ish-ta' oo oo-rah'ree-oo

Have you a time-table?   Tem um horário?
ten oon oo-rah'ree-oo

What does this sign mean?   Que quer dizer este sinal?
kĕ kair dee-zayr' aysht see-nal'

Week-days only.   Só nos dias úteis.
so noozh dee'ăz oo'tay-eesh

On Saturdays.   Aos sábados.
owsh sa'bă-doosh

On Sundays.   Aos domingos.
owzh doo-meen'goosh

On (Bank) holidays.   Em dias feriados.
en dee'ăsh fĕ-ree-ah'doosh

Our luggage is in the station.   A nossa bagagem está na estação.
ă no'să bă-gah'zhen ish-ta' nă ish-tă-sown'

Single to Oporto (first-class, second-class)   Porto (primeira, segunda).
(pohr'too pree-may'ee-ră, sĕ-goon'dă)

Three returns to Oporto.   Três de ida e volta para o Porto.
traysh dee'dă ee vol'tă pă'roo pohr'too

And two halves (*i.e. two half fares*) for the children.   E dois meios para as crianças.
ee doh'eezh may'yoosh pă-rash' kree-an'săsh

How much is that?   Quanto é?
kwan'too e

For how long is this ticket valid?   Qual é a validade deste bilhete?
kwal e ă vă-lee-dahd' day ht bee-lyayt'

I want to reserve a seat (two seats) in the nine-fifteen to . . .   Quero reservar um lugar no comboio das nove e quinze para . . .
kair'oo rĕ-zĕr-var' oon loo-gar' noo kon-boy'oo dăzh nov ee keenz pă'ră . . .

Facing the engine.	Voltado para a máquina.

vohl-tah'doo pă-rah' ma'kee-nă

Back to the engine.	De costas para a máquina.

dě kosh'tăsh pă-rah' ma'kee-nă

A window seat.	Um lugar à janela.

oon loo-gar' ah zhă-ne'lă

Non-smoking.	Não fumadores.

nown foo-mă-doh'rěsh

In the front, middle, back of the train.	À frente, a meio, na cauda do comboio.

ah frent, ă may'yoo, nă kow'dă doo kon-boy'oo

Is there a dining car?	Há vagão-restaurante?

ah vă-gown' rěsh-tow-rant'

Is there a sleeping car?	Há carruagem-cama?

ah kă-roo-ah'zhen kă'mă

Can I reserve a sleeping berth?	Posso reservar uma cama?

po'soo rě-zěr-var' oo'mă kă'mă

Upper (lower) berth.	Uma cama de cima (de baixo).

oo'mă kă'mă dě see'mă (dě bў'shoo)

There are no seats left.	Não há lugares.

nown ah loo-garsh'

When do we arrive in . . . ?	Quando chegamos a . . . ?

kwan'doo shě-gă'mooz ă . . .

Can I break my journey in . . . ?	Posso interromper a viagem em . . . ?

po'soo een-tě-ron-payr' ă vee-ah'zhen en . . .

Must I change (trains)?	Tenho de mudar (de comboio).

te'nyoo dě moo-dar' (dě kon-boy'oo)

Do we change trains at the frontier?	Há trasbordo na fronteira?

ah trăzh-bor'doo nă fron-tay'ee-ră

You have to change at . . .	Tem de mudar em . . .

ten dě moo-dar' en . . .

Is the connection from the same station?	A ligação é da mesma estação.

ă lee-gă-sown' e dă mayzh'mă ish-tă-sown'

How long do I have to wait?	Quanto tempo tenho de esperar?

kwan'too ten'poo te'nyoo dish-pě-rar'

Is there a through train to ...?   Há um comboio directo para ...?
ah oon kon-boy'oo dee-re'too pă'ră ...

Is there a supplementary charge?   Paga-se excesso?
pah'găs eesh-se' soo

Does the train pass through...?   O comboio passa por ...?
oo kon-boy'oo pa'să poor ...

Does it stop at ...?   Pára em ...?
pah'ră en ...

Where is the train for ...?   Onde está o comboio para ...?
ond ish-ta' oo kon-boy'oo pă'ră ...

When does the train for ... leave?   Quando parte o comboio para ...?
kwan'doo part oo kon-boy'oo pă'ră ...

From which platform?   Qual é a linha? (De que cais?)
kwal e ă lee'nyă (dĕ kĕ kỹsh)

I am in a hurry.   Tenho pressa.
te'nyoo pre'să

I don't want to miss the train.   Não quero perder o comboio.
nown kair'oo pĕr-dayr' oo kon-boy'oo

Has the train for ... gone?   Já partiu o comboio para ...?
zhah păr-tee'oo oo kon-boy'oo pă'ră ...

I've missed the train for ...   Perdi o comboio para ...
pĕr-dee' oo kon-boy'oo pă'ră ...

How long shall I have to wait?   Quanto (tempo) tenho de esperar?
kwan'too (ten'poo) te'nyoo dish-pĕ-rar'

Is there another train this morning (this afternoon, this evening)?   Há outro comboio esta manhã (à tarde, esta noite)?
ah oh'troo kon-boy'oo esh'tă mă-nyan' (ah tard, esh'tă noh'eet)

Am I in the right train for ...?   É este o comboio para ...?
e aysht oo kon-boy'oo pă'ră ...

The last train has gone.   O último comboio já saiu.
oo ool'tee-moo kon-boy'oo zhah să-yoo'

What should I do then?   Que devo fazer nesse caso?
kĕ day'voo fă-zayr' nays kah'zoo

Is this seat free (vacant)?	Este lugar está livre?
	aysht loo-gar' ish-ta' leev'rĕ
Is there room for two here?	Há aqui lugar para dois?
	ah ă-kee' loo-gar' pă'ră doh'eesh
That seat is taken.	Esse lugar está ocupado.
	ays loo-gar' ish-ta' oo-koo-pah'doo
I reserved a seat.	Reservei um lugar.
	rĕ-zĕr-vay'ee oon loo-gar'
Excuse me, that seat is mine.	Desculpe, esse lugar é meu.
	dish-koolp', ays loo-gar' e may'oo
Where is the ticket collector?	Onde está o revisor?
	ond ish-ta' oo rĕ-vee-zohr'
What is the matter?	Que se passa?
	kĕ sĕ pa'să
Excuse me (= may I pass?).	Dá-me licença; com licença.
	da'mĕ lee-sen'să; kon lee-seen'să
Put my luggage on the rack.	Ponha a minha bagagem n rede.
	poh'nya mee'nyă bă-gah'zhen nă rayd
I am sorry to disturb you.	Desculpe incomodá-lo (*fem* -la).
	dish-koolp' een-koo-moo-da'loo (-lă)
Are these things in your way?	Estas coisas incomodam?
	esh'tăsh koh'ee-zăz een-koo-mo'down
No, it's quite all right.	Não, não incomodam.
	nown, nown een-koo-mo'down
Do you mind if I smoke?	Importa-se que fume?
	een-por'tă-sĕ kĕ foom
Can you give me a light, please?	Pode dar-me lume, se faz favor
	pod dar'mĕ loom, sĕ fash fă-vohr'
Would you like to see the paper?	Quer ler o jornal?
	kair layr oo zhoor-nal'
May I open the window?	Dá-me licença que abra janela?
	da'mĕ lee-sen'să kee ab'ra zhă-ne'lă
Would you mind if I have the window closed?	Importa-se que feche a janela
	een-por'tăs kĕ fesh ă zhă-ne'lă

The window will not close, open.   A janela não fecha, abre.
ă zhă-ne'lă nown fay'shă, ab'rĕ

The door is jammed.   A porta não abre.
ă por'tă nown ab'rĕ

Do you feel a draught?   Sente uma corrente de ar?
sent oo'mă koo-rent' dar

It is hot, cold.   Está quente, frio.
ish-ta' kent, free'oo

Is the sun troubling you?   O sol incomoda-o?
oo sol een-koo-mo'dă-oo

We can draw the blind.   Podemos baixar (correr) as cortinas.
poo-day'moozh bỹ-shar' (koo-rayr') ăsh koor-tee'năsh

Is there a bell for the attendant?   Há uma campainha para chamar o empregado?
ah oo'mă ka-npă-een'yă pă'ră shă-mar' oo en-prĕ-gah'doo

I should like something to drink.   Queria qualquer coisa para beber.
kĕ-ree'ă kwal'kair koh'ee-ză pă'ră bĕ-bayr'

What are we stopping for?   Porque é que paramos?
poor'kee e kĕ pă-ră'moosh

How much longer is it to . . . ?   Quanto demora até . . . ?
kwan'too dĕ-mo'ra ă-te' . . .

What station is this?   Que estação é esta?
kee ish-tă-sown' e esh'tă

How long does the train stop here?   Quanto tempo pára o comboio aqui?
kwan'too ten'poo pah'ră oo kon-boy'oo ă-kee'

Can I get out?   Posso sair?
po'soo să-eer'

Have I time to go to the refreshment room?   Tenho tempo para ir ao bufete?
te'nyoo ten'poo pă'ră eer ow boo-fayt'

Where is the refreshment room?   Onde é o bufete (o restaurante, a cantina)?
on'dee e oo boo-fayt' (oo rĕsh-tow-rant', ă kan-tee'nă)

Are we nearly at . . . ?   Estamos perto de . . . ?
ish-tă'moosh pair'too dĕ . . .

Are we late? Vamos atrasados?
vă'mooz ă-tră-zah'doosh

We are on time. Vamos à tabela.
vă'mooz ah tă-be'lă

Where are we now? Onde estamos agora?
ond ish-tă'mooz ă-go'ră

Do you know whether we pass Sabe se passamos por . . . ?
through . . . ?
sab sĕ pă-să'moosh poor . . .

Here is my ticket. Aqui está o meu bilhete.
ă-kee' ish-ta' oo may'oo bee-lyayt'

To pull the communication cord. Puxar o sinal de alarme.
poo-shar' oo see-nal' da-larm'

MOTORING

It is advisable to join the AA or RAC as they provide expert advice and
service to motorists travelling abroad. Tyre pressures are measured by the
UK standard.

VOCABULARY
For Road Signs see p. 136

by car, de carro (dĕ ka'roo), de automóvel (đow-too-mo'vel)
accelerator, o acelerador (ă-sĕ-lĕ-ră-dohr')
axle, o eixo (ay'shoo)
back-axle, o eixo traseiro (ay'shoo tră-zay'ee-roo)
battery, a bateria (bă-tĕ-ree'ă)
body, a carrossaria (kă-roo-să-ree'ă)
bolt, uma cavilha (kă-vee'lyă)
bonnet, o capot (kă-poh')
boot, a mala (ma'lă)
brake, o travão (tră-vown'), o freio (fray'yoo)
brakes, os travões (tră-voynsh') os freios (fray'yoos)
breakdown, uma panne (pan)
breakdown lorry, o reboque (rĕ-bok')
bulb, a lâmpada (lan'pă-dă)
bumper, o pára-choques (pa'ră shoksh)
bus, o autocarro (ow-too-ka'roo)
can (petrol), uma lata (la'tă)
cap (radiator), o tampão (tan-pown')
car, o carro (ka'roo), o automóvel (ow-too-mo'vel)
caravan, a roulotte (roo-lot'), a caravana (kără-vă'nă)

carburettor, o carburador (kăr-boo-ră-ḋohr')
check, to, ver (vayr), examinar (ee-ză-mee-nar')
choke, o ar (ar)
clean, to, limpar (leen-par')
clutch, a embraiagem (en-brỹ-ah'zhen)
dipstick, a vareta do óleo (vă-ray'tă doo o'lee-oo)
door, a porta (por'tă)
drive, to, guiar (gee-ar')
driver, o condutor (kon-doo-tohr')
driving licence, a carta de condução (kar'tă dĕ kon-doo-sown')
engine, o motor (moo-tohr')
exhaust, o tubo de escape (too'boo dĕsh-kap')
fan, a ventoinha (ven-too-ee'nyă)
fan-belt, a correia da ventoinha (koo-ray'yă dă ven-too-ee'nyă)
fill, to, encher (en-shayr')
fine, uma multa (mool'tă)
funnel, o funil (foo-neel')
garage, a garagem (gă-rah'zhen), a estação de serviço (ish-tă-sown' dĕ sĕr-vee'soo)
gear (first, second, third, fourth), a velocidade (vĕ-loo-see-dahd') primeira, segunda, terceira, quarta (pree-may'ee-ră, sĕ-goon'dă, tĕr-say'ee-ră, kwar'tă)
gear-box, a caixa de velocidades (kỹ'shă dĕ vĕ-loo-see-ḋahḋsh')
gear-lever, a alavanca das mudanças (ă-lă-van'kă dăzh moo-dan' săsh)
handle (door-), o puxador (poo-shă-ḋohr')
highway code, o código da estrada (ko'dee-goo dă ish-trah'dă)
horn, a buzina (boo-zee'nă)
hub, o tampão (tan-pown')
ignition, a ignição (eeg-nee-sown')
ignition key, a chave de ignição (shahv ḋeeg-nee-sown')
indicator (direction-), o pisca-pisca (peesh'kă peesh'kă)
inner tube, a câmara (de ar) (kă'mă-ră dar)
insurance policy, a apólice de segurança (ă-po'lees dĕ sĕ-goo-ran'să)
jack, o macaco (mă-ka'koo)
key, a chave (shahv)
leak, uma fuga (foo'gă)
lever, a manivela (mă-nee-ve'lă)
licence, a licença (lee-sen'să)
lights (dipped), os médios (me'dee-oosh)
lights (head-), os máximos (ma'see-moosh)
lights (rear), as luzes de trás (loo'zĕsh dĕ trash)
lights (side-), os mínimos (mee'nee-moosh)
lock, o fecho (fay'shoo)
lorry, o camião (kă-mee-own')
lubrication, a lubrificação (loo-bree-fee-kă-sown')
map, o mapa (ma'pă)
mechanic, o mecânico (mĕ-kă'nee-koo)
mirror, o espelho (ish-pay'lyoo)
motor-cycle, a motocicleta (moo-too-see-kle'tă)

motorway, a autoestrada (ow-too-ish-trah'dă)
mudguard, o guarda-lamas (gwar'dă lă'măsh)
number-plate, a chapa de matrícula (sha'pă dě mă-tree'koo-lă)
nut, uma porca (pohr'kă)
oil, o óleo (o'lee-oo)
park, to, estacionar (ish-tă-see-oo-nar')
parking, estacionamento (ish-tă-see-oo-nă-men'too)
pedestrian, um peão (pee-own')
petrol, a gasolina (gă-zoo-lee'nă)
petrol pump, a bomba de gasolina (bon'bă dě gă-zoo-lee'nă)
petrol station, um posto de gasolina (pohsh'too dě gă-zoo-lee'nă)
plug, uma vela (ve'lă)
pump, uma bomba (bon'bă)
puncture, um furo (foo'roo)
rack (roof-), o porta-bagagens (por'tă bă-ga'zhensh)
radiator, o radiador (ră-dee-ă-dohr')
rear-window, a janela de trás (zhă-ne'lă dě trash)
repairs, as reparações (rě-pă-ră-soynsh')
reverse, a marcha-atrás (mar-sha-trash')
roof, o tejadilho (tě-zhă-dee'lyoo)
scooter, uma scooter (skoo'tair)
screw, um parafuso (pă-ră-foo'zoo)
seat, o assento (ă-sen'too)
skid, to, derrapar (dě-ră-par')
spanner, uma chave de porcas (shahv de pohr'kăsh)
spare parts, peças sobresselentes (pe'săsh soh-brě-să-lentsh')
speed, a velocidade (vě-loo-see-dahd')
speed-limit, o limite de velocidade (lee-meet' dě vě-loo-see-dahd')
speedometer, o conta-quilómetros (kontă kee-lo'mě-troosh)
spring, a mola (mo'lă)
start, to, pôr em marcha (pohr en mar'shă)
starter, o démarreur (de-ma-ray')
steering-wheel, o volante (voo-lant')
stop, to, parar (pă-rar')
swerve, to, guinar (gee-nar')
switch, o interruptor (een-tě-roop-tohr')
tank, o depósito (dě-po'zee-too)
traffic, o tráfego (tra'fě-goo)
traffic jam, um engarrafamento (en-gă-ră-fă-men'too)
traffic lights, as luzes de trânsito (loo'zěsh dě tran'zee-too)
trailer, o reboque (rě-bok')
tram, o eléctrico (ee-le'tree-koo)
transmission, a transmissão (tranzh-mee-sown')
tyre, o pneu (pnay'oo)
tyre pressure, a pressão dos pneus (prě-sown' doosh pnay'oosh)
unscrew, to, desapertar (dě-ză-pěr-tar')
valve, uma válvula (val'voo-lă)
van (tradesman's), uma carrinha (kă-ree'nyă)
vehicle, um veículo (vay-ee'koo-loo)
wash, to, lavar (lă-var')

washer, uma anilha (ă-nee'lyă)
water, a água (ag'wă)
water (distilled), água destilada (ag'wă dish-tee-lah'dă)
wheel, a roda (ro'dă)
wheel (back-), a roda de trás (ro'dă dĕ trash)
wheel (front-), a roda de frente (ro'dă dĕ frent)
wheel (spare), a roda sobressalente (ro'dă soh-brĕ-să-lent')
windscreen, o para-brisas (pa'ră bree'zăsh)
windscreen-wiper, o limpa-vidros (leen'pă vee'droosh)

need petrol (oil, water). Preciso de gasolina (óleo, água).

prĕ-see'zoo dĕ gă-zoo-lee'nă (o'lee-oo, ag'wă)

Give me . . . litres. Dê-me . . . . litros.

day'mĕ . . . lee'troosh

Fill up the tank. Encha o depósito.

en'shă oo dĕ-po'zee-too

Will you please check the tyres ? Veja a pressão dos pneus, por favor.

vay'zhă ă prĕ-sown' doosh pnay'oosh, poor fă-vohr'

Check the water. Veja a água.

vay'zhă ag'wă

My car is up there (not far; perhaps a kilometre from here). O meu carro está ali (perto; talvez um quilómetro de aqui).

oo may'oo ka'roo ish-ta' ă-lee' (pair'too; tal-vayz' oon kee-lo'mĕ-troo dă-kee')

Have you got a can (and a funnel)? Tem uma lata (e um funil)?

ten oo'mă la'tă ee oon foo-neel'

There is something wrong with my car. Há qualquer avaria no meu carro.

ah kwal'kair ă-vă-ree'ă noo may'oo ka'roo

I don't know what is wrong. Não sei qual é a avaria.

nown say'ee kwal e a-vă-ree'ă

The trouble seems to be here. A avaria parece ser aqui.

a-vă-ree'ă pă-res' sayr ă-kee'

This doesn't work. Isto não funciona.

eesh'too nown foon-see-oh'nă

There is a leak here. Há aqui uma fuga.

ah ă-kee' oo'mă foo'gă

The engine won't start.	O motor não pega.
	oo moo-tohr' nown pe'gã
The clutch is sticking.	A embraiagem está colada.
	ã en-brỹ-ah'zhen ish-ta' koo-lah'dã
Do you do repairs?	Fazem reparações?
	fa'zen rĕ-pă-ră-soynsh'
Can you repair . . . ?	Pode reparar . . . ?
	pod rĕ-pă-rar' . . .
How long will it take?	Quanto tempo demorará?
	kwan'too ten'poo dĕ-moo-rĕ-ra'
Can I leave the car here?	Posso deixar o carro aqui?
	po'soo day-shar' oo ka'roo ă-kee'
Where is the manager?	Onde está o patrão?
	ond ish-ta' oo pă-trown'
How much will it cost, approximately?	Quanto custará, aproximadamente?
	kwan'too koosh-tă-ra', ă-pro-see-ma-dă-ment'
When does the garage open?	Quando abre a garagem?
	kwan'doo ab'rĕ ă gă-rah'zhen
The car needs to be overhauled.	O carro precisa duma revisã completa.
	o ka'roo prĕ-see'zã doo'mã rĕ-vee-zown' kon-ple'tã
This must be straightened (replaced).	Isto precisa de ser endireitad (substituído).
	eesh'too prĕ-see'zã dĕ sayr en-dee-ray-tah'doo (soobsh-tee-too-ee'doo)
This is out of position.	Isto está fora do lugar.
	eesh'too ish-ta' fo'rã doo loo-gar'
This is broken.	Isto está partido.
	eesh'too ish-ta' păr-tee'doo
My car is in a ditch.	O meu carro está numa valet
	oo may'oo ka'roo ish-ta' noo'mã vă-lay'tã
Is there a breakdown service?	Há serviço de reboque?
	ah sĕr-vee'soo dĕ rĕ-bok'
My car is damaged.	O meu carro está avariado.
	oo may'oo ka'roo ish-ta' ă-vă-ree-ah'doo
Can you lend me . . . ?	Pode-me emprestar . . . ?
	pod'mee en-prĕsh-tar'

an you give me a tow, please? Pode dar-me reboque, por favor?

pod dar'mě rě-bok', poor fǎ-vohr'

an you give me a lift, please? Pode dar-me boleia, por favor?

pod dar'mě boo-le'yǎ, poor fǎ-vohr'

have lost my documents. Perdi os meus papéis.

pěr-dee' oozh may'oosh pǎ-pe'eesh

have lost my way. Perdi-me.

pěr-dee'mě

Which is the way to . . . ? Qual é o caminho para . . . ?

kwal e oo kǎ-mee'nyoo pǎ'rǎ . . .

ow far is it to . . . ? Qual é a distância até . . . ?

kwal e ǎ deesh-tan'see-ǎ ǎ-te' . . .

ACCIDENTS

here has been an accident. Houve um desastre.

ohv oon dě-zash'trě

rst-aid post. O posto de socorros.

oo pohsh'too dě soo-ko'roosh

e need a doctor, ambulance. Precisamos de um médico, de uma ambulância.

prě-see-zǎ'moosh doon me'dee-koo, doo'mǎ an-boo-lan'see-ǎ

all a policeman. Chame um polícia.

sham oon poo-lee'see-ǎ

elp! Socorro!

soo-koh'roo

uickly! Depressa!

dě-pre'sǎ

e (she) is badly hurt. Ele (ela) está gravemente ferido (*fem.* ferida).

ayl (e'lǎ) ish-ta' grah-vě-ment' fě-ree'doo (fě-ree'dǎ)

e (she) has been knocked down. Foi atropelado (*fem.* atropelada).

foh'ee ǎ-troo-pě-lah'doo (ǎ-troo-pě-lah'dǎ)

ave you any bandages? Tem ligaduras?

ten lee-gǎ-doo'rǎsh

Help me to carry him (her).   Ajude-me a levá-lo (-la).
       ă-zhoo'dĕ-mĕ ă lĕ-va'loo (-'lă)

Don't move him (her)!   Não lhe mexam!
       nown lyĕ may'shown

We need a stretcher.   Precisamos duma maca.
       prĕ-see-ză'moosh doo'mă ma'kă

Careful!   Cuidado!
       kwee-dah'doo

I am all right.   Estou bem.
       ish-toh' ben

It is not serious.   Não é grave.
       nown e grahv

That hurts.   Isso dói.
       ee'soo doy

Gently.   Com jeito.
       kon zhay'ee-too

Who is responsible for the accident?   De quem é a culpa do desastr
       dĕ ken e ă kool'pă doo dĕ-zash'trĕ

It was (not) my fault.   A culpa (não) foi minha.
       ă kool'pă (nown) foh'ee mee'nyă

It is his (her) fault.   A culpa é dele (dela).
       ă kool'pă e dayl (de'lă)

He was driving too fast.   Ele ia a muita velocidade.
       ayl ee'ah mween'tă vĕ-loo-see-dahd'

He overtook me on the bend.   Ultrapassou-me na curva.
       ool-tră-pă-soh'mĕ nă curva

He was on the wrong side of the road.   Ia fora de mão.
       ee'ă fo'ră dĕ mown

The car skidded (swerved).   O carro derrapou (guinou).
       oo ka'roo dĕ-ră-poh' (gee-noh')

I did not see (understand) the sign (signal).   Não vi (percebi) o sinal.
       nown vee (pĕr-sĕ-bee') oo see-nal'

I don't understand.   Não percebo.
       nown pĕr-say'boo

am British (English), American.   Sou inglês (*fem.* inglesa), americano (*fem.* americana).

soh een-glaysh' (een-glay'ză),
ă-mĕ-ree-kă'noo (ă-mĕ-ree-kă'nă)

ere is my driving licence (my   Aqui está a minha carta de
passport).   condução (o meu passaporte)

ă-kee' ish-ta' ă mee'nyă kar'tă dĕ kon-doo-sown' (oo may'oo pă-să-port')

am not used to driving here yet.   Ainda não estou acostumado a
guiar aqui.

ă-een'dă nown ish-toh' ă-koosh-too-mah'doo ă gee-ar' ă-kee'

CUSTOMS, PORTERS, LUGGAGE

VOCABULARY

bag, a mala (ma'lă)
baggage, a bagagem (bă-gah'zhen)
basket, o cesto (saysh'too)
binoculars, os binóculos (bee-no'koo-loosh)
bottle, uma garrafa (gă-rah'fă)
box, a caixa (kў'shă)
camera, a máquina (fotográfica) (ma'kee-nă foo-too-gra'fee-kă)
case, a mala (ma'lă)
cigar, o charuto (shă-roo'too)
cigarette, o cigarro (see-ga'roo)
Customs, a Alfândega (al-fan'dĕ-gă)
customs officer, o funcionário de Alfândega (foon-see-oo-nah'ree-oo
dal-fan'dĕ-gă)
declare, to, declarar (dĕ-klă-rar')
document, o documento (doo-koo-men'too)
duty, os direitos (dee-ray'ee-toosh)
form, um impresso (een-pre'soo)
frontier, a fronteira (fron-tay'ee-ră)
handbag, a carteira (de senhora) (kăr-tay'ee-ră dĕ sĕ-nyoh'ră)
item (of luggage), o volume (voo-loom')
jewellery, joalharia (zhoo-ă-lyă-ree'ă)
key, a chave (shahv)
label, o rótulo (ro'too-loo)
luggage, a bagagem (bă-gah'zhen)
number, o número (noo'mĕ-roo)
object, o objecto (ob-zhe'too)
package, o pacote (pă-kot')
parcel, o embrulho (en-broo'lyoo)
passport, o passaporte (pa-să-port')
piece (of luggage), o volume (voo-loom')

porter, o bagageiro (bă-gă-zhay'ee-roo)
present, um presente (pré-zent')
quantity, a quantidade (kwan-tee-dahd')
receipt, o recibo (ré-see' boo)
receipt (for luggage), a senha (say'nyă)
spirits, os espiritos (ish-pee'ree-toosh)
suitcase, a mala (ma'lă)
tobacco, o tabaco (tă-ba'koo)
trunk, mala grande (ma'lă grand)
visa, um visto (veesh'too)
wine, o vinho (vee'nyoo)

Where is the customs? Onde é a Alfândega?
ond'ee e al-fan'dĕ-gă

Where are the passports ex- Onde são vistos os passaportes
amined?
ond sown veesh'tooz oosh pa-să-portsh'

Here is my passport. Aqui está o meu passaporte.
ă-kee' ish-ta' oo may'oo pa-să-port'

How much money have you? Quanto dinheiro tem?
kwan'too dee-nyay'ee-roo ten

I have ... pounds, escudos. Tenho ... libras, escudos.
te'nyoo ... lee'brăsh, ish-koo'doosh

I have ... in travellers' cheques. Tenho ... em cheques de vi-
jante.
te'nyoo ... en sheksh dĕ vee-ă-zhant'

I am waiting for the customs Estou à espera do funcionári
officer.
ish-toh' ah ish-pair'ă doo foon-see-oo-nah'ree-oo

This is my luggage. Esta é a minha bagagem.
esh'tă e ă mee'nyă bă-gah'zhen

These are all mine. Tudo isto é meu.
too'doo eesh'too e may'oo

Have you anything to declare? Tem alguma coisa a declara
ten al-goo'mă koh'ee-ză ă dĕ-klă-rar'

Please open your cases. Faz favor de abrir as suas mala
fash fă-vohr' dă-breer' ăsh soo'ăzh ma'lăsh

I can't open this case. Não sou capaz de abrir es
mala.
nown soh kă-pazh' dă-breer' esht'tă ma'lă

The lock is stuck.	A fechadura está estragada.
	ă fĕ-shă-doo'ră ish-ta' ish-tră-gah'dă
I have lost the key.	Perdi a chave.
	pĕr-dee' ă shahv
For my personal use.	Para meu uso pessoal.
	pă'ră may'oo oo'zoo pĕ-soo-al'
I am a tourist.	Sou turista.
	soh too-reesh'tă
I am here on holiday.	Estou aqui de férias.
	ish-toh' ă-kee' dĕ fe'ree-ăsh
It is a business visit.	É uma visita de negócios.
	e oo'mă vi-zee'tă dĕ nĕ-go'see-oosh
I am staying here for a fortnight.	Fico aqui quinze dias.
	fee'koo ă-kee' keenz dee'ăsh
It has been used.	É já usado.
	e zhah oo-zah'doo
I have only bought a few things during my stay.	Comprei apenas algumas coisas durante a minha visita.
	kon-pray'ee ă-pay'năz al-goo'măsh koh'ee-zăzh doo-rant' ă mee-nyă vi-zee'tă
Is this dutiable?	Isto paga direitos?
	eesh'too pah'gă dee-ray'ee-toosh
How much must I pay?	Quanto tenho que pagar?
	kwan'too te'nyoo kĕ pă-gar'
Where do I pay?	Onde pago?
	ond pah'goo
Have you finished?	Já acabou?
	zhah ă-kă-boh'
Have the cases been marked?	As malas já foram marcadas?
	ăzh ma'lăzh zhah foh'rown măr-kah'dăsh
My luggage has been examined.	A minha bagagem já foi examinada.
	ă mee'nyă bă-gah'zhen zhah foh'ee ee-ză-mee-nah'dă
I am in a hurry.	Estou com muita pressa.
	ish-toh' kon mween'tă pre'să
Are you free?	Está livre?
	ish-ta' leev'rĕ
Take my luggage.	Leve a minha bagagem.
	lev ă mee'nyă bă-gah'zhen

Can you carry this case too?	Pode levar esta mala também?
	pod lĕ-var' esh'tă ma'lă tan-ben'
I shall take this myself.	Eu levo isto.
	ay'oo le'voo eesh'too
It is not mine.	Não é meu.
	nown e may'oo
It is broken.	Está partido.
	ish-ta' păr-tee'doo
Be careful with this case.	Cuidado com esta mala.
	kwee-dah'doo kon esh'tă ma'lă
I have some heavy luggage too.	Também tenho bagagem pesada.
	tan-ben' te'nyoo bă-gah'zhen pĕ-zah'dă
Four pieces.	Quatro volumes.
	kwa'troo voo-loomsh'
Where can I leave my luggage?	Onde posso guardar as malas?
	ond po'soo gwăr-dar' ăzh ma'lăsh
Left luggage office.	O depósito de bagagem.
	oo dĕ-po'zee-too dĕ bă-gah'zhen
Where can I register the luggage?	Onde posso despachar a bagagem?
	ond po'soo dish-pă-shar' ă bă-gah'zhen
Can I take these things in the compartment with me?	Posso levar estas coisas no compartimento comigo?
	po'soo lĕ-var' esh'tăsh koh'ee-zăzh noo kon-păr-tee-men'too koo-mee'goo
Put them here.	Ponha-as aqui.
	poh'nyaz ă-kee'
I want to send these cases in advance.	Quero mandar estas malas com antecedência.
	kair'oo man-dar' esh'tăzh ma'lăsh kon an-tĕ-sĕ-den'see-ă
I want to insure my luggage.	Quero segurar a minha bagagem.
	kair'oo sĕ-goo-rar' ă mee'nyă bă-gah'zhen
What does it cost?	Quanto custa?
	kwan'too koosh'tă
It is not worth while.	Não vale a pena.
	nown val ă pay'nă

Where can I find you? — Onde o posso encontrar?
ond'ee oo po'soo en-kon-trar'

Wait for me here. — Espere aqui por mim.
ish-pair' ă-kee' poor meen

I am going to the refreshment room. — Vou ao restaurante.
voh ow rĕsh-tow-rant'

I shall be back soon; in ten minutes. — Volto já; daqui a dez minutos.
vol'too zhah; dă-kee' ă dezh mi-noo'toosh

I shall wait for you on the platform; at the entrance. — Espero-o no cais; à entrada.
ish-pair'oo-oo noo kÿsh; ah en-trah'dă

Can you get me a taxi? — Pode-me chamar um táxi?
pod'mĕ shă-mar' oon tak'see

Where are the taxis? — Onde estão os táxis?
ond ish-town' oosh tak'seesh

AT THE LEFT-LUGGAGE

I wish to leave these things here. — Quero deixar estas coisas aqui.
kair'oo day-shar' esh'tăsh koh'ee-zăz ă-kee'

Until about four o'clock. — Até por volta das quatro.
ă-te' poor vol'tă dăsh kwa'troo

Three cases, a raincoat, this parcel, these books. — Três malas, uma gabardina, este pacote, estes livros.
trayzh ma'lăsh, oo'mă gă-băr-dee'nă, aysht pă-kot', ayshtzh leev'roosh

How much is there to pay? — Quanto é?
kwan'too e

How much do you charge for each item? — Quanto custa cada volume?
kwan'too koosh'tă kă'dă voo-loom'

Do I pay now or when I collect the things? — Pago agora ou quando levar as coisas?
pah'goo ă-go'ră oh kwan'doo lĕ-var' ăsh koh'ee-zăsh

Those are my things over there. — As minhas coisas estão ali.
ăzh mee'nyăsh koh'ee-zăz ish-town' ă-lee'

There is one case missing.　Falta uma mala.
　　　　　　　　　　fal'tă oo'mă ma'lă

Where is the parcel?　Onde está o pacote?
　　　　　　　　ond ish-ta' oo pă-kot'

This is not mine.　Isto não é meu.
　　　　　　　eesh'too nown e may'oo

I want to take out one suitcase.　Quero levar uma mala.
　　　　　　　　　　　kair'oo lĕ-var' oo'mă ma'lă

The remainder can stay.　O resto pode ficar.
　　　　　　　　　oo resh'too pod fee-kar'

This case is not locked.　Esta mala não está fechada à
　　　　　　　　　　chave.
　　　　　esh'tă ma'lă nown ish-ta' fĕ-shah'dă ah shahv

The lock is broken.　A fechadura está quebrada.
　　　　　　　ă fĕ-shă-doo'ră ish-ta' kĕ-brah'dă

Something has fallen out.　Caiu qualquer coisa.
　　　　　　　　kă-yoo' kwal'kair koh'ee-ză

Please keep an eye on my things　Faz favor de olhar pela minha
till I find a porter.　　　　bagagem enquanto procuro
　　　　　　　　　　　um bagageiro.
fash fă-vohr' dee ohl-yar' pĕ'lă mee'nyă bă-gah'zhen en-kwan'too proo-koo'roo oon
　　　　　　　　bă-gă-zhay'ee-roo

TOURS, EXCURSIONS, SEASIDE

VOCABULARY

art gallery, o museu de arte (moo-zay'oo dart)
attendant (in museum), o guarda (gwar'dă), empregado (en-prĕ-gah' doo)
avenue, a avenida (ă-vĕ-nee'dă)
bathe, to, tomar um banho (too-mar' oon bă'nyoo)
bathing cap, uma touca de banho (toh'kă dĕ bă'nyoo)
bathing costume, um fato de banho (fah'too dĕ bă'nyoo)
bathing tent (hut, cabin), uma barraca (de praia) (bă-rah'kă (dĕ prÿ'ă))
bay, a baía (bă-ee'ă)
beach, a praia (prÿ'ă)
beach-guard, o cabo-de-mar (kah'boo dĕ mar)

boat, o barco (bar'koo)
book, um livro (leev'roo)
book, to, reservar (rĕ-zĕr-var')
bridge, a ponte (po*n*t)
bucket, um balde (bald)
building, um edifício (ĕ-dee-fee'see-oo)
buoy, uma boia (boy'ă)
canoe, uma canoa (kă-noh'ă)
castle, o castelo (kăsh-te'loo)
cathedral, a catedral (kă-tĕ-dral')
channel, o canal (kă-nal')
church, a igreja (ee-gray'zhă)
cliff, a falésia (fă-le'zee-ă)
coast, a costa (kosh'tă)
current, a corrente (koo-re*n*t')
danger, o perigo (pĕ-ree'goo)
deck-chair, uma cadeira de praia (kă-day'ee-ră dĕ prỹ'ă)
diving-board, a prancha de saltos (pra*n*'shă dĕ sal-toosh)
excursion, uma excursão (ish-koor-sow*n*')
ferry, o ferry (fe'ree)
fish, o peixe (pay'eesh)
fish, to, pescar (pĕsh-kar')
garden, o jardim (zhăr-dee*n*')
gate, o portão (poor-tow*n*')
guide, o guia (gee'ă)
guide book, o guia (gee'ă)
hill, o outeiro (oh-tay'ee-roo)
house, a casa (kah'ză)
information centre, (tourist), o centro de turismo (se*n*'troo dĕ too-reezh'moo)
interpreter, o intérprete (ee*n*-tair'prĕt)
lake, o lago (lah'goo)
lighthouse, o farol (fă-rol')
monastery, o mosteiro (moosh-tay'ee-roo), o convento (ko*n*-ve*n*'too)
monument, o monumento (moo-noo-me*n*'too)
motor-boat, o barco a motor (bar'koo ă moo-tohr')
mountain, a montanha (mo*n*-tă'nyă)
mountain range, a serra (se'ră)
museum, o museu (moo-zay'oo)
path, a vereda (vĕ-ray'dă)
promenade, a avenida marginal (ă-vĕ-nee'dă măr-zhee-nal')
raft, a jangada (zha*n*-gah'dă)
reef, o escolho (ish-koh'lyoo)
river, o rio (ree'oo)
road, a estrada (ish-trah'dă)
rock, o rochedo (roo-shay'doo)
rowing boat, um barco a remos (bar'koo a ray'moosh)
sailing boat, um barco à vela (bar'koo ah ve'lă)
sand, a areia (ă-ray'yă)
sandhill, a duna (doo'nă)

sea, o mar (mar)
seashell, a concha (kon'shă)
seaside, a praia (prỹ'ă)
shade (cover), um toldo (tohl'doo)
spade (child's), uma pàzinha (pah-zee'nyă)
square, a praça (prah'să)
street, a rua (roo'ă)
sun, o sol (sol)
sunglasses, os óculos de sol (o'koo-loozh dě sol)
sunshade, um toldo (tohl'doo)
swim, to, nadar (nă-dar')
swimming pool, a piscina (peesh-see'nă)
tide, a maré (mă-re')
tide (high), a preia-mar (pray'yă mar)
tide (low), a baixa-mar (bỹ'shă mar)
tour, a excursão (ish-koor-sown')
tourist, o (a) turista (too-reesh'tă)
translate, to, traduzir (tră-doo-zeer')
water-skiing, o esqui-aquático (ish-kee' ă-kwa'tee-koo)
wave, o onda (on'dă)
way, o caminho (kă-mee'nyoo)

Have you a list of excursions (tours).	Tem uma lista de excursões?
	ten oo'mă leesh'tă dish-koor-soynsh'
How much is this trip?	Quanto é esta excursão?
	kwan'too e esh'tă ish-koor-sown'
I want two seats for the excursion to . . . on Friday.	Quero dois lugares para a excursão a . . . na sexta-feira
	kair'oo doh'eesh loo-garsh' pra ish-koor-sown' ă . . . nă saysh'tă fay'ee-ră
What time does it leave?	A que horas parte?
	ă kee o'răsh part
When do we get back?	A que horas estaremos de volta?
	ă kee o'răz ish-tă-ray'moozh dě vol'tă
Is lunch included?	O almoço está incluído?
	oo al-moh'soo ish-ta' een-kloo-ee'doo
Is there an English-speaking guide?	Há um guia que fale inglês?
	ah oon gee'ă kě fal een-glaysh'
I want a guide book, a map, of the city.	Queria um roteiro, um mapa da cidade.
	kě-ree'ă oon roo-tay'ee-roo, oon ma'pă, dă see-dahd'

Have you one in English? Tem uma edição em inglês?
ten oo'mă ee-dee-zown' en een-glaysh'

Excuse me, can you tell me the Fazia favor, podia indicar-me
way to . . . ? o caminho para . . . ?
fă-zee'ă fă-vohr', poo-dee'ă een-dee-kar'mee oo kă-mee'nyoo pă'ră . . .

Is this the right way to . . . ? É este o caminho para . . . ?
e aysht oo kă-mee'nyoo pă'ră . . .

Is it a good road? A estrada é boa?
ă ish-trah'dă e boh'ă

How do I get from here to . . . ? Como se vai daqui a . . . ?
koh'moo sĕ vỹ dă-kee' ă . . .

I am lost. Perdi-me.
pĕr-dee' mĕ

We want to get to . . . Queremos ir a . . .
kĕ'ray'mooz eer ă . . .

I am looking for . . . Procuro . . .
proo-koo'roo . . .

Is it far? É longe?
e lonzh

How long does it take? Quanto tempo leva?
kwan'too ten'poo le'vă

Is it better to go by taxi, tram, É preferível ir de táxi, de eléc-
bus? trico, de autocarro?
e prĕ-fĕ-ree'vel eer dĕ tak'see, dee-le'tree-koo, dow-too-ka'roo

Where is the tram stop, bus stop? Onde é a paragem do eléctrico,
do autocarro?
on'dee e ă pă-rah'zhen doo ee-le'tree-koo, doo ow-too-ka'roo

Does this bus, tram, go to . . . ? Este autocarro, eléctrico, vai
para . . . ?
aysht ow-too-ka'roo, ee-le'tree-koo, vỹ pă'-ră . . .

Is this the terminus? É a última paragem?
e ă ool'tee-mă pă-rah'zhen

Do I have to change? Tenho de mudar?
te'nyoo dĕ moo-dar'

Which way? Em que direcção?
en kĕ dee-re-sown'

Straight ahead. Sempre em frente.
sen'pren frent

To the right, left.　　　À direita, à esquerda.
　　　ah dee-ray'ee-tă, ah ish-kayr'dă

First turning on the right.　　A primeira rua (=street
　　　　　　　estrada (=road) à direita.
　　　ă pree-may'ee-ră roo'ă (ish-trah'dă) ah dee-ray'ee-tă

Second turning on the left.　　A segunda rua à esquerda.
　　　ă sĕ-goon'dă roo'ă ah ish-kayr'dă

I want to hire a car.　　Queria alugar um carro.
　　　kĕ-ree'ă ă-loo-gar' oon ka'roo

For the day.　　Para o dia inteiro.
　　　pă'ră oo dee'ă een-tay'ee-roo

How much is it per day?　　Quanto é por dia?
　　　kwan'too e poor dee'ă

How much is it per hour?　　Quanto é por hora?
　　　kwan'too e poor o'ră

Have you got a driver who speaks Tem um condutor que fa
　English?　　　　　inglês?
　　　ten oon kon-doo-tohr' kĕ fal een-glaysh'

We want to tour the district.　Queremos dar uma volta pela
　　　　　　　região.
　　　kĕ-ray'moozh dar oo'mă vol'tă pĕ'lă rĕ-zhee-own'

We want to go to . . .　　Queremos ir a . . .
　　　kĕ-ray'mooz eer ă . . .

Stop here (there).　　Pare aqui (ali).
　　　par ă-kee' (ă-lee')

Stop at the corner.　　Pare na esquina.
　　　par nă ish-kee'nă

More slowly, please.　　Mais devagar, por favor.
　　　mўzh dĕ-vă-gar', poor fa-vohr'

Where can we have lunch?　　Onde podemos almoçar?
　　　ond poo-day'mooz al-moo-sar'

Pick us up at the hotel　　Vá buscar-nos ao hotel
　(the boarding house).　　　(à pensão).
　　　va boosh-kar'nooz ow oh-tel' (ah pen-sown')

Can you come at 10 o'clock?　Pode vir às dez?
　　　pod veer azh desh

e must be back by (not later than) 5 o'clock.

Temos de estar de volta o mais tardar às cinco.

tay'moozh dish-tar' dĕ vol'tă oo mỹzh tăr-dar' ash seen'koo

must be back before 6 o'clock.

Tenho de estar de volta antes das seis.

te'nyoo dish-tar' dĕ vol'ta antsh dăsh say'eesh

want to see all that is worth seeing.

Queria ver tudo quanto valha a pena ver.

kĕ-ree'ă vayr too'doo kwan'too va'lya pay'nă vayr

ave we time to see . . . ?

Temos tempo para ver . . . ?

tay'moosh ten'poo pă'ră vayr . . .

ave only two hours to spare.

Só tenho duas horas disponíveis.

so te'nyoo doo'ăz o'răzh deesh-poo-nee'vaysh

hat street, church, is this?

Que rua, igreja, é esta?

kĕ roo'ă, ee-gray'zhă, e esh'tă

hat building is that?

Que edifício é aquele?

kee ĕ-dee-fee'see-oo e ă-kayl'

hat is that?

Que é aquilo?

kee e ă-kee'loo

m interested in art galleries, museums.

Tenho interesse nos museus de arte, museus históricos.

e'nyoo een-tĕ-rays' noozh moo-zay'oozh dart, moo-zay'ooz eesh-to'ree-koosh

want to see the cathedral, the town hall, the university, the Roman remains, the tiled walls.

Queria ver a catedral, o município, a universidade, as ruínas romanas, os azulejos.

ree'ă vayr ă kă-tĕ-dral', oo moo-nee-see'pee-oo, ă oo-nee-vĕr-see-dahd', ăzh roo-ee'năzh roo-mă'năsh, ooz ă-zoo-lay'zhoosh

hould like to visit the botanic gardens, the zoo.

Queria visitar o jardim botânico, o jardim zoológico.

ree'ă vi-zee-tar' oo zhăr-deen' boo-tă'nee-koo, oo zhăr-deen' zoo-lo'zhee-koo

it worth getting out?

Vale a pena sair?

val ă pay'nă să-eer'

ait here.

Espere aqui.

ish-pair' ă-kee'

it open?

Está aberto?

ish-ta' ă-bair'too

When does it open, close?   Quando abre, fecha?
kwa*n*'doo ab'rĕ, fay'shã

Can one see over the church, the castle?   Pode-se visitar a igreja, castelo?
pod'sĕ vi-zee-tar' ă ee-gray'zhã, oo kăsh-te'loo

To whom does one apply for permission to enter?   A quem se pede licença pa entrar?
ă ke*n* sĕ ped lee-se*n*'să pă'ră e*n*-trar'

Can we go around alone?   Podemos ir sòzinhos?
poo-day'mooz eer so-zeen'yoosh

Do we need a guide?   Precisamos dum guia?
prĕ-see-ză'moozh doo*n* gee'ă

When does the next tour start?   Quando começa a próxi visita?
kwa*n*'doo koo-me'să ă pro'see-mă vi-zee'tă

How long does it take?   Quanto tempo leva?
kwa*n*'too te*n*'poo le'vă

How long must we wait?   Quanto tempo temos de esperar?
kwa*n*'too te*n*'poo tay'moozh dish-pĕ-rar'

I am not interested in that.   Isso não me interessa.
ee'soo now*n* mĕ ee*n*-tĕ-re'să

How much further have we to go?   Até onde devemos ir?
ă-te' o*n*d dĕ-vay'mooz eer

How many rooms, steps, are there?   Quantas salas, quantos degra há?
kwa*n*'tăsh sa'lăsh, kwa*n*'toozh dĕ-growsh', ah

Is there a good view?   Há bonitas vistas?
ah boo-nee'tăsh veesh'tăsh

May I take a photograph here?   Posso tirar uma fotografia aqui?
po'soo tee-rar' oo'mă foh-too-grã-fee'ă ă-kee'

Please stop a moment.   Faz favor de parar um mo ento.
fash fă-vohr' dĕ pă-rar' oo*n* moo-me*n*'too

Is this the . . . memorial?   Este é o monumento de . . .
aysh'tee e oo moh-noo-me*n*'too dĕ . . .

here is . . . buried? Onde está enterrado . . . ?
o*n*d ish-ta' e*n*-tĕ-rah'doo . . .

here did . . . live? Onde morava . . . ?
o*n*d moo-rah'vă . . .

hat is the name of that? Como se chama aquilo?
koh'moo sĕ shă'mă ă-kee'loo

ow much is the catalogue? Quanto custa o catálogo?
kwa*n*'too koosh'tă oo kă-ta'loo-goo

an I buy any picture postcards? Posso comprar postais ilustrados?
po'soo ko*n*-prar' poosh-tȳz' ee-loosh-trah'doosh

ave you a book about . . . ? Tem um livro sobre . . . ?
te*n* oo*n* leev'roo soh'brĕ . . .

oes one have to walk? É preciso ir a pé?
e prĕ-see'zoo eer ă pe

it close by? É perto?
e pair'too

et us go. Vamos.
vă'moosh

am tired. Estou cansado.
ish-tọh' ka*n*-sah'doo

et us rest a bit. Vamos descansar um pouco.
vă'moozh dĕsh-ka*n*-sar' oo*n* poh'koo

is too hot. Faz muito calor.
fazh mwee*n* too kă-lohr'

have seen enough for today. Já vi bastante por hoje.
zhah vee băsh-ta*n*t' poor ohzh

here can I get some refresh- Onde posso tomar uns refres-
ments? cos?
o*n*d po'soo too-mar' oonzh rĕ-fraysh'koosh

is going to rain. Vai chover.
vȳ shoo-vayr'

Where can we shelter? Onde podemos encontrar ab-
rigo?
o*n*d poo-day'mooz e*n*-ko*n*-trar' ă-bree'goo

an we get a taxi? Podemos tomar um táxi?
poo-day'moosh too-mar' oo*n* tak'see

Which is the best way back?	Qual é o melhor caminho de regresso?
	kwal e oo měl-yor' kǎ-mee'nyoo dě rě-gre'soo

Drive through ...	Vá por ...
	va poor ...

Drive back as quickly as possible.	Volte o mais depressa possível
	volt oo mỹzh dě-pre'sǎ poo-see'vel

How much ought I to give the guide?	Quanto devo dar ao guia?
	kwan'too day'voo dar ow gee'ǎ

Thank you very much.	Muito obrigado.
	mweent oh-bree-gah'doo

Are you free tomorrow?	Está livre amanhã?
	ish-ta' leevr a-mǎ-nyan'

Can you come at ten?	Pode vir às dez?
	pod veer azh desh

Which is the way to the beach?	Qual é o caminho para a praia
	kwal e oo kǎ-mee'nyoo prah prỹ'ǎ

Is it a pebbly beach?	Há muitas pedras na praia?
	ah mween'tǎsh pe'drǎsh nǎ prỹ'ǎ

Is it easy to get there?	O caminho para lá é fácil?
	oo kǎ-mee'nyoo pǎ'rǎ lah e fah'seel

Can one park near the beach?	Pode-se estacionar o carro ao pé da praia?
	pod'sě ish-tǎ-see-oo-nar' oo ka'roo ow pe dǎ prỹ'ǎ

Where can we bathe?	Onde se pode tomar banho?
	ond sě pod too-mar' bǎ'nyoo

Is it safe?	Não há perigo?
	nown ah pě-ree'goo

Is it safe for children?	Não há perigo para as crianças
	nown ah pě-ree'goo prash kree-an'sǎsh

Is the water shallow (deep)?	A água é baixa (funda)?
	ag'wǎ e bỹ'shǎ (foon'dǎ)

Are there dangerous currents (channels)?	Há correntes perigosas (can perigosos)?
	ah koo-rentsh' pě-ree-go'zǎsh (kǎ-nỹsh' pě-ree-go'zoosh)

I can't swim (very well).   Não sei nadar (muito bem).
nown say'ee nă-dar' (mween'too ben)

I should like to go for a swim.   Gostava de tomar um banho.
goosh-tah'vă dĕ too-mar' oon bă'nyoo

I want to hire a tent (cabin).   Quero alugar uma barraca.
kair'oo ă-loo-gar' oo'mă bă-ra'kă

I should like to go for a sail.   Gostava de dar um passeio num barco à vela.
goosh-tah'vă dĕ dar oon pă-say'yoo noon bar'koo ah ve'lă

Where is the attendant?   Onde está o banheiro?
ond ish-ta' oo bă-nyay'ee-roo

What is the charge?   Quanto custa?
kwan'too koosh'tă

Are my things safe here?   As minhas coisas estão em segurança aqui?
ăzh mee'nyăzh koh'ee-zăsh ish-town' en sĕ-goo-ran'să ă-kee'

Where can we get a drink?   Onde podemos beber qualquer coisa?
ond poo-day'moozh bĕ-bayr' kwal'kair koh'ee-ză

I have lost (she has lost, we have lost).   Perdi (ela perdeu, perdemos).
pĕr-dee' (e'lă pĕr-day'oo, pĕr-day'moosh) ...

Can you help me?   Pode ajudar-me?
pod ă-zhoo-dar'mĕ

Help!   Socorro!
soo-koh'roo

Come quickly!   Venha depressa!
ve'nyă dĕ-pre'să

Someone is in difficulties.   Está alguém atrapalhado.
ish-ta' algen' ă-tră-pă-lyah'doo

Somebody is drowning.   Está ali uma pessoa a afogar-se.
ish-ta' ă-lee' oo'mă pĕ-soh'ă a-foo-gar'sĕ

Hold on! Hold tight!   Segure-se! Aguente-se!
sĕ-goo'rĕ-sĕ; ă-gwen'tĕ-sĕ

Catch hold!   Apanhe!
ă-pa'nyĕ

VISITING FRIENDS

I am looking for number ...	Procuro o número ... proo-koo′roo oo noo′mĕ-roo ...
Does Mr. Costa live here?	O senhor Costa mora aqui? oo sĕn-yohr′ kosh′tă mo′ră ă-kee′
Is he at home?	Está em casa? ish-tă′ en kah′ză
I am ...	Eu sou ... ay′oo soh ...
Tell him it is ...	Diga-lhe que é ... dee′gă-lyĕ kee e ...
Here is my card.	Aqui está o meu cartão. ă-kee′ ish-ta′ oo may′oo kăr-town′
Please come in.	Faz favor de entrar. fash fă-vohr′ den-trar′
He will be in at ...	Volta às ... vol′tă ash ...
He won't be long.	Não deve tardar muito. nown dev tăr-dar′ mween′too
Could you come back at ... ?	Podia voltar às ... ? poo-dee′ă vohl-tar′ ash ...
Would you please wait a moment.	Tenha a bondade de esperar um momento. ten′ya bon-dahd dish-pĕ-rar′ oon moo-men′too
Please tell him I called.	Faz favor de lhe dizer que estive aqui. fash fă-vohr′ dĕ lyĕ dee-zayr′ kee ay′oo ish-teev′ ă-kee′
Mr. ... asked me to call on you.	O senhor ... pediu-me para o visitar. oo sĕn-yohr′ ... pĕ-dee′oo-mĕ pă′ră oo vi-zee-tar′
How do you do?	Muito prazer (em conhecê-lo). mween′too pră-zayr′ (en koo-nyĕ-say′loo)
I speak very little Portuguese.	Falo pouco português. fa′loo poh′koo poor-too-gaysh′

Do you speak English (French, Spanish)?
Fala inglês (francês, espanhol)?
fa'lă een-glaysh', fran-saysh', ish-pă-nyol'

I believe ... has mentioned my name to you.
Creio que ... já lhe mencionou o meu nome.
kray'yoo kĕ ... zhah lyĕ men-see-oo-noh' oo may'oo nohm

I have a letter of introduction.
Tenho uma carta de apresentação.
te'nyoo oo'mă kar'tă dă-prĕ-zen-tă-sown'

He is a good friend of mine.
É muito meu amigo.
e mween'too may'oo ă-mee'goo

I have known him for a long time.
Conheço-o há muito tempo.
koo-nyay'soo-oo ah mween'too ten'poo

I knew him in ...
Conheci-o em ...
koo-nyĕ-see'oo en ...

He sends you his greetings.
Manda-lhe cumprimentos.
man'dă-lyĕ koon-pree-men'toosh

May I introduce ... ?
Dá-me licença que lhe apresente ... ?
da'-mĕ lee-sen'să kĕ lyĕ ă-prĕ-zent' ...

My wife, my husband, my son, my daughter, my friend.
Minha mulher, meu marido, meu filho, minha filha, um amigo meu.
meen'yă moo-lyair', may'oo mă-ree'doo, may'oo fee'lyoo, mee'nyă fee'lyă, oon ă-mee'goo may'oo

My uncle, my aunt.
Meu tio, minha tia.
may'oo tee'oo, mee'nyă tee'ă

My nephew, niece.
Meu sobrinho, minha sobrinha.
may'oo soo-bree'nyoo, mee'nyă soo-bree'nyă

My cousin (male, female).
Meu primo, minha prima.
may'oo pree'moo, mee'nyă pree'mă

My brother-in-law, sister-in-law.
Meu cunhado, minha cunhada.
may'oo koo-nyah'doo, mee'nyă koo-nyah'dă

Could you come at ... ?
Podia vir às ... ?
poo-dee'ă veer ash ...

I should like to very much.
Teria muito prazer.
tĕ-ree'ă mween'too pră-zayr'

I shall come to the hotel, boarding house.	Eu irei ao hotel, à pensão.

ay'oo ee-ray'ee ow oh-tel', ah pen-sown'

Please do not go to any trouble.	Não se incomode.

nown see een-koo-mod'

I hope it is not inconvenient.	Espero que não seja inoportuno.

ish-pair'oo kĕ nown say'zhă ee-noo-poor-too'noo

Here is the address.	Aqui está a direcção.

ă-kee' ish-ta' ă dee-re-sown'

I shall be glad to help you, accompany you, invite you.	Terei muito prazer em ajudá-lo, acompanhá-lo, convidá-lo.

tĕ-ray'ee mween'too pră-zayr' en ă-zhoo-da'loo, ă-kon-pă-nya'loo, kon-vee-da'loo

Good-bye.	Adeus.

ă-day'oosh

My greetings to your wife.	Cumprimentos à sua senhora.

koon-pree-men'tooz ah soo'ă sĕ-nyoh'ră

Until later.	Até logo.

ă-te' lo'goo

Until we meet again.	Até à vista.

ă-te' ah veesh'tă

Until tomorrow.	Até amanhã.

ă-te' a-mă-nyan'

THE HOTEL OR BOARDING HOUSE

The cost of rooms and meals in hotels and boarding houses are, or should be, posted in the rooms as well as in the hall or entrance of each establishment. Prices in Portugal are moderate, though rising, by British standards. Accommodation is not usually hard to find. Lists of hotels and boarding houses can be obtained from the "Casa de Portugal" in London or the Comissariado do Turismo in Lisbon.

Sample letter for booking a room in advance:

> Dear Sir,
> *I wish to reserve one/two, etc. single/double room(s) (with bath) for . . . night(s) from the . . . (date) to the . . . (date). I shall be glad if you will let me have a note of the cost.*
>   *Yours faithfully,*

Exmo. Senhor,

 Pode, por favor, reservar-me um/dois, etc. quarto(s) (de uma cama/de casal) (com banho) por . . . noite(s), a começar em . . . e até . . .

 Agradeceria que me informasse acerca do preço.

  Com os meus cumprimentos

VOCABULARY

ashtray, um cinzeiro (seen-zay'ee-roo)
bath, o banho (bă'nyoo)
bathroom, a casa de banho (kah'ză dĕ bă'nyoo)
bed, a cama (kă'mă)
bed (double), uma cama de casal (kă'mă dĕ kă-zal'
bedroom, o quarto (kwar'too)
bed and breakfast, dormida e pequeno almoço (door-mee'dă ee pĕ-kay'noo al-moh'soo)
bell, a campainha (kan-pă-ee'nyă)
bill, a conta (kon'tă)
blanket, o cobertor (koo-bĕr-tohr'
blind, a cortina (koor-tee'nă)
blind (venetian), a persiana (pĕr-see-ă'nă)
board (full), pensão completa (pen-sown' kon-ple'tă)
boarding house, uma pensão (pen-sown')
bolster, o travesseiro (tră-vĕ-say'ee-roo)
book, to, reservar (rĕ-zĕr-var')
breakfast, o pequeno almoço (pĕ-kay'noo al-moh'soo)
bulb (light), uma lâmpada (lan'pă-dă)
chair, uma cadeira (kă-day'ee-ră)
chest of drawers, uma cómoda (ko'moo-dă)
clothes, a roupa (roh'pă)
coat-hanger, um cabide (kă-beed')
cook, o cozinheiro (koo-zee-nyay'ee-roo)
cupboard, o armário (ăr-mah'ree-oo)
curtain, a cortina (koor-tee'nă)
dining room, a sala de jantar (sa'lă de zhan-tar'
dinner, o jantar (zhan-tar')
door, a porta (por'tă)
drawer, uma gaveta (gă-vay'ta)
dressing-table, o toucador (toh-kă-dohr')
eiderdown, o edredão (e-drĕ-down')
floor (storey), o andar (an-dar')
form (document), uma ficha (fee'shă)
glass (for water etc.), um copo (ko'poo)
heating, o aquecimento (ă-ke-see-men'too)
hotel, o hotel (oh-tel')
iron, to, passar a ferro (pă-sar' ă fe'roo)
key, a chave (shahv)
lamp, uma lâmpada (lan'pă-dă)

landing, o patamar (pă-tă-mar′)
landlady, a dona da casa (doh′nă dă kah′ză)
latch, o trinco (treen′koo)
laundry, a lavandaria (lă-van-dă-ree′ă)
lavatory, a casa de banho (kah′ză dĕ bă′nyoo); a toilette (twa-let′)
   o lavatório (lă-vă-to′ree-oo)
lift, o elevador (ee-lĕ-vă-dohr′)
light, a luz (loosh)
lock, a fechadura (fĕ-shă-doo′ră)
lounge, o salão (să-lown′)
lunch, o almoço (al-moh′soo)
maid, a criada (kree-ah′dă)
management, a gerência (zhĕ-ren′see-ă)
manager, o gerente (zhĕ-rent′)
mattress, o colchão (kohl-shown′)
meal, uma refeição (rĕ-fay-sown′)
mirror, o espelho (ish-pay′lyoo)
napkin, um guardanapo (gwar-dă-na′poo
office, o escritório (ish-kree-to′ree-oo)
page-boy, o 'groom' (groom)
pail, um balde (bald)
picnic lunch, um lanche (lansh)
pillow, uma almofada (al-moo-fah′dă)
plug (of washbasin), a tampa (tan′pă)
plug (electric), uma ficha (fee′shă)
porter, o porteiro (poor-tay′ee-roo)
pot (chamber-), um bacio (bă-see′oo)
press, to, (button), carregar em (kă-rĕ-gar′ en)
proprietor, o dono (doh′noo)
pull, to, puxar (poo-shar′)
push, to, empurrar (en-poo-rar′)
radiator, o irradiador (ee-ră-dee-ă-dohr′)
reading lamp, um candeeiro (kan-dee-ay′roo)
reception desk, a recepção (rĕ-se-sown′)
reservation, a reserva (rĕ-zair′vă)
ring, to, (bell), tocar (too-kar′)
sheet, o lençol (len-sol′)
shelf, a prateleira (pră-tĕ-lay′ee-ră)
shower, o duche (doosh)
shutters, as gelosias (zhĕ-lo-zee′ăsh)
sitting room, a sala de estar (sa′lă dish-tar′)
soap, o sabonete (să-boo-nayt′)
stairs, a escada (ish-kah′dă)
switch (light), o interruptor (een-tĕ-roop-tohr′)
table, a mesa (may′ză)
tap, a torneira (toor-nay′ee-ră)
tap, hot-water, torneira de água quente (dag′wă kent
tap, cold-water, torneira de água fria (dag′wă free′ă)
tea, o chá (shah)
terrace, a esplanada (ish-plă-nah′dă), o terraço (tĕ-ra′soo

towel, a toalha (too-a'lyă)
tray, a bandeja (ban-day'zhă), o tabuleiro (tă-boo-lay'ee-roo)
veranda, a varanda (vă-ran'dă)
waiter, o criado (kree-ah'doo)
wardrobe, o guarda-roupa (gwar'dă roh'pă)
washbasin, a bacia (bă-see'ă)
washstand, o lavatório (lă-vă-to'ree-oo)
waste-paper basket, um cesto de papéis (saysh'too đe pă-pe'eesh)
window, a janela (zhă-ne'lă)

an you recommend a hotel, a   Pode recomendar um hotel,
  boarding house?   uma pensão?
        pod rě-koo-men-dar' oon oh-tel', oo'mă pen-sown'

want to be near the centre of   Quero ficar perto do centro da
  the town.   cidade.
        kair'oo fee-kar' pair'too doo sen'troo dă see-dahd'

don't want to be in a noisy area.   Não quero ficar num sítio baru-
                                    lhento.
        nown kair'oo fee-kar' noon see'tee-oo bă-roo -lyen'too

Where is the . . . hotel   Onde é o hotel (pousada,
  ('pousada', 'estalagem')?   estalagem) . . .?
        on'dee e oo oh-tel' (poh-zah'dă, ish-tă-lah'zhen

Where is the reception desk?   Onde é a recepção?
        on'dee e ă rĕ-se-sown'

Where is the office?   Onde é o escritório?
        on'dee e oo ish-kree-to'ree-oo

Where is the manager?   Onde está o gerente?
        ond ish-ta' oo zhĕ-rent'

am Mr. (Mrs., Miss) . . .   Sou o senhor (a senhora) . . .
        soh oo sĕ-nyohr' (ă sĕ-nyoh'ra) . . .

wrote to reserve accommo-   Escrevi para reservar um
  dation.   quarto (quartos).
        ish-krĕ-vee' pă'ră rĕ-zĕr-var' oon kwar'too (kwar'toosh)

idn't you get my letter?   Não recebeu a minha carta?
        nown rĕ-sĕ-bay'oo ă mee'nyă kar'tă

wrote five weeks ago.   Escrevi há cinco semanas.
        ish-krĕ-vee' ah seen'koo sĕ-mă'năsh

wanted a room for two nights.   Queria um quarto por duas
                                noites.
        kĕ-ree'ă oon kwar'too poor doo'ăsh noh'eetsh

Have you a room vacant?   Tem um quarto livre?

ten oon kwar'too lee'vrĕ

Have you accommodation for tonight?   Tem quartos para esta noite

ten kwar'toosh pără esh'tă noh'eet

Can I have a room for the night?   Arranjam-me um quarto pa esta noite?

ă-ran'zhown-mĕ oon kwar'too pă'ră esh'tă noh'eet

We wanted to stay for a week, perhaps longer.   Queríamos ficar uma sema talvez mais.

kĕ-ree' ă-moosh fee-kar' oo'mă sĕ-mă'nă, tal-vayzh' mỹsh

I want a room for my wife and myself.   Queria um quarto para min minha mulher.

kĕ-ree'ă oon kwar'too pă'ră meen ee mee'nyă moo-lyair'

And a room for the children.   E um quarto para as criang ([older children] os menino

ee oon kwar'too prash kree-an'săsh (oozh mĕ-nee'noosh)

A room for my son (my daughter).   Um quarto para meu fil (minha filha).

oon kwar'too pă'ră may'oo fee'lyoo (mee'nyă fee'lyă)

We can sleep in the same room.   Podemos dormir no mes quarto.

poo-day'moozh door-meer' noo mayzh'moo kwar'too

Have you a room on the ground floor (on the first floor)?   Tem um quarto no rés-do-ch (no primeiro andar)?

ten oon kwar'too noo rezh'doo-shown (noo pree-may'-ee-roo an-dar')

Just bed and breakfast.   Só dormida e pequeno almo

so door-mee'dă ee pĕ-kay'noo al-moh'soo

With full board.   Com pensão completa.

kon pen-sown' kon-ple'tă

What do you charge?   Quais os preços?

kwỹz oosh pray'soosh

We shall have lunch out.   Almoçamos fora.

al-moo-să'moosh fo'ră

We should like a meal in the evening.   Queríamos uma refeição noite.

kĕ-ree'ă-mooz oo'mă rĕ-fay-sown' ah noh'eet

Have you a room with a private bathroom? | Tem um quarto com casa de banho?
ten oon kwar'too kon kah'ză dĕ bă'nyoo

Is there a lift? | Tem elevador?
ten ee-lĕ-vă-dohr'

May I see the room? | Posso ver o quarto?
po'soo vayr oo kwar'too

I want a quiet room. | Quero um quarto sossegado (tranquilo).
kair'oo oon kwar'too soo-sĕ-gah'doo (tran-kwee'loo)

I do not like this room. | Não gosto deste quarto.
nown gosh'too daysht kwar'too

Have you another room available? | Tem outro quarto livre?
ten oh'troo kwar'too lee'vrĕ

It is too noisy here. | Aqui é muito barulhento.
ă-kee' e mween'too bă-roo-lyen'too

I can't sleep; there is too much noise. | Não posso dormir; há muito barulho.
nown po'soo door-meer'; ah mween'too bă-roo'lyoo

The traffic (the radio) keeps me awake. | O tráfego (o rádio) não me deixa dormir.
oo trá'fĕ-goo (oo rah'dee-oo) nown mĕ day'ee-shă door-meer'

Have you a room at the front, at the back? | Tem algum quarto na frente, nas traseiras?
ten al-goon' kwar'too nă frent, năsh tră-zay'ee-răsh

I shall have to find another place. | Tenho que procurar outro lugar.
te'nyoo kĕ proo-koo-rar' oh'troo loo-gar'

This is too small. | É muito pequeno.
e mween'too pĕ-kay'noo

Have you nothing else? | Não tem mais nada?
nown ten mўzh nah'dă

I'll take this room. | Fico com este quarto.
fee'koo kon aysht kwar'too

What is the number of the room? | Qual é o número do quarto?
kwal e oo noo'mĕ-roo doo kwar'too

Have you got the key?　　　Tem a chave?
　　　　　　　　　　　　　　　ten ă shahv

Please have the luggage brought　Faz favor de mandar a bagag-
to our room.　　　　　　em para o nosso quarto.
　　fash fă-vohr' dě man-dar' ă bă-gah'zhen pă'ră oo no'soo kwar'too

Please open the windows.　　Faz favor de abrir as janelas.
　　　　fash fă-vohr' dă-breer' ăzh zhă-ne'lăsh

How do I open this window?　Como se abre esta janela?
　　　　koh'moo see a'brě esh'tă zhă-ne'lă

How does this work?　　　　Como funciona isto?
　　　　koh'moo foon-see-oh'nă eesh'too

Where is the bell?　　　　　Onde é a campainha?
　　　　on'dee e ă kan-pă-ee'nyă

Where have you put our things?　Onde é que pôs as nossas coisas?
　　　on'dee e kě pohz ăs no'săsh koh'ee-zăsh

Where is the bathroom (the　Onde é a casa de banho?
lavatory)?
　　　　on'dee e ă kah'ză dě bă'nyoo

Where is the lounge, dining　Onde é o salão, a sala de jantar,
room, bar?　　　　　　o bar?
　　　on'dee e oo să-lown', ă sa'lă dě zhan-tar', oo bar

Do you serve tea?　　　　　Servem chá?
　　　　　sair'ven shah

I am going out now.　　　　Vou sair agora.
　　　voh să-eer' ă-go'ră

I shall be back for lunch, for　Volto para o almoço, o jantar.
dinner.
　　　vol'too pă'ră oo al-moh'soo, oo zhan-tar'

Please bring some (drinking)　Traga-me água (para beber),
water.　　　　　　　　por favor.
　　　trah'gă-mě a'gwă (pă'ră bě-bayr'), poor fă-vohr'

Can one drink the water from the　A água da torneira pode-se
tap?　　　　　　　　beber?
　　　ag'wă dă toor-nay'ee-ră pod'sě bě-bayr'

Please bring some soap, a towel,　Faz favor de trazer sabonete
hot water.　　　　　　uma toalha, água quente.
　　fash fă-vohr' dě tră-zayr' să-boo-nayt', oo'mă too-a'lyă, a'gwă kent

Please get a bath ready for me.   Faz favor de me preparar um banho.
fash fă-vohr' dĕ mĕ prĕ-pă-rar' oon bă'nyoo

Call me at eight o'clock.   Chame-me às oito.
sha'mĕ-mĕ az oh'ee-too

Good night.   Boa noite.
boh'ă noh'eet

Good morning.   Bom dia.
bon dee'ă

Who is there?   Quem é?
ken e

Come in.   Entre.
en'trĕ

What time is it?   Que horas são?
kee o'răsh sown

Wait a moment.   Espere um momento.
ish-pair' oon moo-men'too

Can I have my shoes cleaned?   Posso mandar limpar os meus sapatos?
po'soo man-dar' leen-par' oozh may'oosh să-pah'toosh

I should like my clothes brushed, pressed.   Queria a minha roupa escovada, passada a ferro.
kĕ-ree'ă mee'nyă roh'pă ish-koo-vah'dă, pă-sah'dă ă fe'roo

Are there any letters for me?   Há correspondência para mim?
ah koo-rĕsh-pon-den'see-ă pă'ră meen

Has anyone asked for me?   Perguntou alguém por mim?
prĕ-goon-toh' al-gen' poor meen

Did anyone telephone for me?   Telefonou-me alguém?
tĕ-lĕ-foo-noh'mĕ al-gen'

I want to post a letter.   Quero pôr uma carta no correio.
kair'oo pohr oo'mă kar'tă noo koo-ray'yoo

Have you any stamps?   Tem selos?
ten say'loosh

I want to go to . . .   Quero ir a . . .
kair'oo eer ă . . .

How do I get there?   Como se vai lá?
koh'moo sĕ vỹ lah

Can I get something to eat (drink) when I return? Posso comer (beber) alguma coisa ao voltar?
po'soo koo-mayr' (bĕ-bayr') al-goo'mă koh'ee-ză ow vohl-tar'

Is there a night porter on duty? Há porteiro de serviço à noite?
ah poor-tay'ee-roo dĕ sĕr-vee'soo ah noh'eet

Is ... still in his (her) room? ... está ainda no quarto?
... ish-tah' ă-e'endă noo kwar'too

What is the number of the room? Qual é o número do quarto?
kwal e oo noo'mĕ-roo doo kwar'too

Will you send a message to him (her)? É capaz de lhe mandar um recado?
e kă-pazh' dĕ lyĕ man-dar' oon rĕ-kah'doo

I should like some tickets for the cinema. Queria bilhetes para o cinema.
kĕ-ree'ă beel-yetsh' pă'ră oo see-nay'mă

What time does it begin? A que horas começa?
ă kee o'răsh koo-me'să

I wish to pay my bill. Queria pagar a minha conta.
kĕ-ree'ă pă-gar' ă mee'nyă kon'tă

How much is it? Quanto é?
kwan'too e

What are these charges for? Do que são estas verbas?
doo kĕ sown esh'tăzh vair'băsh

I think there is a mistake here. Creio que há um engano aqui.
kray'yoo kee ah oon en-gă'noo ă-kee'

I did not have ... Não tive ...
nown teev ...

You said the rooms cost ... Disse que os quartos custavam ...
dees kee oosh kwar'toosh koosh-tah'vown ...

May I have the receipt? Pode dar-me o recibo?
pod dar'mee oo rĕ-see'boo

Do I tip, or is there a charge for service in the bill? Devo dar uma gorjeta, ou está incluído o serviço na conta?
day'voo dar oo'mă goor-zhay'tă, oh ish-ta' een-kloo-ee'doo oo sĕr-vee'soo nă kon'tă

I am leaving tomorrow, tonight, this afternoon. Saio amanhã, esta noite, esta tarde.
sỹ'oo a-mă-nyan', esht'tă noh'eet, esh'tă tard

Will you have my luggage brought down? — Poderia mandar trazer a minha bagagem?

poo-dĕ-ree'ă man-dar' tră-zayr' ă mee'nyă bă-gah'zhen

Send the luggage to the station. — Mande a bagagem à estação.

mand ă bă-gah'zhen ah ish-tă-sown'

How soon should I leave? — A que horas devo sair?

ă kee o'răzh day'voo să-eer'

How long does it take to the station, the dock, the airport? — Quanto tempo se demora daqui à estação, ao cais, ao aeroporto?

wan'too ten'poo sĕ de-mo'ră dă-kee' ah ish-tă-sown', ow kysh, ow air-oo-pohr'too

Can I walk? — Posso ir a pé?

po'soo eer ă pe

Please get a taxi. — Faz favor de chamar um táxi.

fash fă-vohr' dĕ shă-mar' oon tak'see

Have you any labels? — Tem etiquetas?

ten e-tee-kay'tăsh

I should like some food for the journey. — Desejava qualquer coisa de comer para a viagem.

dĕ-zĕ-zhah'vă kwal'kair koh'ee-ză dĕ koo-mayr' prah' vee-ah'zhen

When must I leave my room? — Quando devo desocupar o meu quarto?

kwan'doo day'voo dĕ-zoo-koo-par' oo may'oo kwar'too

Can I leave my luggage here? — Posso deixar a minha bagagem aqui?

po'soo day-shar' ă mee'nyă bă-gah'zhen ă-kee'

I have been very comfortable. — Gostei do vosso serviço.

goosh-tay'ee doo vo'soo sĕr-vee'soo

If any letters come for me, please send them to this address:— — Se vier correspondência para mim, faz favor de mandá-la para esta direcção:—

sĕ vee-air' koo-rĕsh-pon-den'see-ă pă'ră meen, fash fă-vohr' dĕ man-da' lă pă'ră esh'tă dee-re-sown'

LAUNDRY AND CLEANING

VOCABULARY

For articles of clothing see under GENERAL SHOPPING VOCABULARY p. 9

clean, to, limpar (leen-par')
cleaner's (dry-), a lavandaria a seco (lă-van-dă-ree'ă ă say'koo)
cleaning (dry-), a limpeza a seco (leen-pay'ză ă say'koo)
clothes, a roupa (roh'pă)
damp, húmido (oo'mee-doo)
dry, seco (say'koo)
dye, to, tingir (teen-zheer')
dyer's, tinturaria (teen-too-ră-ree'ă)
iron, o ferro (fe'roo)
iron, to, passar a ferro (pă-sar' ă fe'roo)
ironing board, a tábua de passar (a ferro) (ta'bwă dĕ pă-sar' ă fe'roo
laundry, a lavandaria (lă-van-dă-ree'ă)
laundry mark, a marca da lavandaria (mar'kă dă lă-van-dă-ree'ă)
mark (stain), uma nódoa (no'dwă)
mend, to, remendar (rĕ-men-dar')
press, to, passar a ferro (pă-sar' ă fe'roo)
soak, to, molhar (moo-lyar')
soap (for laundry), o sabão (să-bown')
soapflakes, os flocos de sabão (flo'koosh dĕ să-bown'
soap powder, o pó de sabão (po dĕ să-bown')
stain, uma nódoa (no'dwă)
starch, a goma (goh'mă)
starch, to, engomar (en-goo-mar')
washing machine, a máquina de lavar (ma'kee-nă dĕ lă-var')
wash, to, lavar (lă-var')
wet, molhado (moo-lyah'doo)

I have some things for washing. Tenho algumas coisas pa
serem lavadas.

te'nyoo al-goo'măsh koh'ee-zăsh pă'ră say'ren lă-vah'dăsh

When will they be ready? Quando estarão prontas?

kwan'doo ish-tă-rown' pron'tăsh

Can I have them by tomorrow Estarão prontas para aman
(by the day after tomorrow)? (para depois de amanhã)?

ish-tă-rown' pron'tăsh pra-mă-nyan' (pă'ră dĕ-poh'eezh da-mă-nyan')

Can I have them by . . . , without Estarão prontas para . . . , se
fail? falta?

ish-tă-rown' pron'tăsh pă'ră . . . , sen fal'tă

e very careful with these.	Tenha muito cuidado com estas coisas.
	te'nyă mween'too kwee-dah'doo kon esh'tăsh koh'ee-zăsh
on't iron this.	Não passe a ferro.
	nown pas ă fe'roo
on't starch the collars.	Não engome os colarinhos.
	nown en-gom' oosh koo-lă-ree'nyoosh
ome of the things need mending.	Algumas coisas precisam de ser remendadas.
	al-goo'măsh koh'ee-zăsh prě-see'zown dě sayr rě-men-dah'dăsh
an you arrange to have them mended?	Pode mandá-las remendar?
	pod man-da'lăzh rě-men-dar'
ere is a vest missing.	Falta uma camisola.
	fal'tă oo'mă kă-mee-zo'lă
ere are three handkerchiefs missing.	Faltam três lenços.
	fal'town trayzh len'soosh
want to send some things for dry cleaning.	Quero enviar algumas coisas para limpeza a seco.
	kair' oo en-vee-ar' al-goo'măsh koh'ee-zăsh pă'ră leen-pay'ză ă say'koo
an you send the laundry to this address, if it isn't ready in time?	Poderia mandar a minha roupa para esta direcção, se não estiver pronta a tempo?
	o-dě-ree'ă man-dar' ă mee'nya roh'pă pă'ră esh'tă dee-re-ksown', sě nown ish-tee-vair' pron'tă ă ten'poo
an this be dyed?	É possível tingir isto?
	e poo-see'vel teen-zheer' eesh'too

RESTAURANT AND CAFÉS

VOCABULARY

GENERAL

ashtray, um cinzeiro (seen-zay'ee-roo)
bar, o bar (bar)
bill, a conta (kon'tă)
bottle, uma garrafa (gă-ra'fă)

bowl, (fruit-), a fruteira (froo-tay'ee-ră)
    (salad-), a saladeira (să-lă-day'ee-ră)
    (soup-), a terrina (tĕ-ree'nă)
café, o café (kă-fe')
coffee-pot, a cafeteira (kă-fĕ-tay'ee-ră)
cork (of bottle), a rolha (roh'lyă)
corkscrew, um saca-rolhas (sa'kă roh'lyăsh)
course (dish), o prato (prah'too)
cup, uma chávena (shah'vĕ-nă)
dinner, o jantar (zhan-tar')
drink, to, beber (bĕ-bayr')
eat, to, comer (koo-mayr')
food, a comida (koo-mee'dă)
fork, o garfo (gar'foo)
glass, um copo (ko'poo); (for Port and liqueurs) um cálice (ka'lees)
hungry, to be, (tayr fom), estar com fome (ish-tar' kon fom)
jug, um jarro (zha'roo)
knife, uma faca (fah'kă)
lunch, luncheon, o almoço (al-moh'soo)
meal, a refeição (rĕ-fay-sown')
menu, a ementa (ee-men'tă), a lista (leesh'tă)
napkin, serviette, o guardanapo (gwar-dă-na'poo)
plate, o prato (prah'too)
restaurant, o restaurante (rĕsh-tow-rant')
saucer, o pires (pee'rĕsh)
spoon, a colher (koo-lyair')
table, a mesa (may'ză)
table-cloth, a toalha de mesa (too-a'lyă dĕ may'ză)
tea, o chá (shah)
teapot, o bule (bool)
thirsty, to be, ter sede (tayr sayd), estar com sede (ish-tar' kon sayd)
tip, uma gorjeta (goor-zhay'tă)
toothpick, um palito (pă-lee'too)
tray, a bandeja (ban-day'zhă), o tabuleiro (tă-boo-lay'ee-roo)
waiter, o criado (kree-ah'doo)
waiter (head), o chefe de mesa (shef dĕ may'ză); o criado-ch
    (kree-ah'doo shef)
waitress, a criada (kree-ah'dă)
wine list, a lista dos vinhos (leesh'tă doozh vee'nyoosh)

FOOD

almonds, as amêndoas (ă-men'doo-ăsh)
apples, as maçãs (mă-sansh)
apricots, os damascos (dă-mash'koosh)
asparagus, o espargo (ish-par'goo)
bananas, as bananas (bă-nă'năsh)
beans (broad), as favas (fah'văsh)
beans (haricot), o feijão verde (fay-zhown' vayrd)
beef (boiled), a carne cozida (karn koo-zee'dă)

beef (roast), a carne assada (karn ă-sah′dä)
beef-steak, um bife (oo*n* beef)
biscuit, uma bolacha (boo-lah′shă)
boiled, cozido (koo-zee′doo)
bread, o pão (oo pow*n*)
broth, o caldo (kal′doo)
butter, a manteiga (ma*n*-tay′ee-gă)
cabbage, a couve (kohv)
cabbage-soup, o caldo verde (kal′doo vayrd)
cake, um bolo (boh′loo)
carrots, as cenouras (sě-noh′răsh)
cauliflower, a couve-flor (ă koh′vě-flohr)
cheese, o queijo (kay′ee-zhoo)
chicken, o frango (fra*n*′goo)
chicken-soup, a canja (de frango) (ka*n*′zhă)
chips, as batatas fritas (bă-ta′tăsh free′tăsh)
chocolate, o chocolate (oo shoo-koo-laht′)
chop (lamb, pork), uma costeleta (de cordeiro, de porco) (koosh-tě-lay′-tă (dě koor-day′ee-roo, dě pohr′koo))
cockles, as amêijoas (ă-may′-zhoo-ăsh)
cod (dried), o bacalhau (bă-kăl-yow′)
cold meat, as carnes frias (karnsh free′ăsh)
crab, o caranguejo (kă-ra*n*-gay′zhoo)
cream, a nata (nah′tă)
cucumber, o pepino (pě-pee′noo)
custard, o creme, a nata (krem, nah′tă)
dates, as tâmaras (tă′mă-răsh)
dessert, a sobremesa (soh-brě-may′ză)
dinner, o jantar (oo zha*n*-tar′)
duck, o pato (pah′too)
eel, a enguia (e*n*-gee′ă)
egg, eggs, o ovo, os ovos (oh′voo, o′voosh)
egg, soft-boiled, hard-boiled, ovo pouco cozido, ovo bem cozido (oh′voo poh′koo koo-zee′doo, oh′voo be*n* koo-zee′doo)
egg, fried, poached, scrambled, ovo estrelado, escalfado, mexido (oh′voo ish-trě-lah′doo, ish-kal-fah′doo, mě-shee′doo)
figs, os figos (fee′goosh)
fish, o peixe (pay′eesh)
fish, fried, boiled, peixe frito, cozido (pay′eesh free′too, koo-zee′doo)
fried, frito (free′too)
fruit, a fruta (froo′tă)
fruit pie, uma empada de fruta (e*n*-pah′dă dě froo′tă)
fruit tart, uma torta de fruta (tor′tă dě froo′tă)
garlic, o alho (al′yoo)
grapes, as uvas (oo′văsh)
gravy, o molho (moh′lyoo)
grilled, grelhado (grě-lyah′doo)
hake, a pescada (pěsh-kah′dă)
ham, o fiambre (oo fee-a*n*′brě)
ham, smoked, o presunto (prě-zoo*n*′too)

herring, o arenque (ă-re*nk*')
hors d'oeuvres, o hors d'oeuvres, os acepipes variados ("hors d'oeuvres", ă-sĕ-peepsh' vă-ree-ah'doosh)
ice, o gelo (zhay'loo)
ice-cream, um gelado, um sorvete (zhĕ-lah'doo, soor-vet')
jam, a compota (de fruta) (ko*n*-po'tă (dĕ froo'tă))
jam (quince), a marmelada (măr-mĕ-lah'dă)
kidney, o rim (oo ree*n*)
lamb, o cordeiro, o borrego (koor-day'ee-roo, boo-ray'goo)
lemon, um limão (lee-mow*n*')
lettuce, a alface (al-fas')
liver, o fígado (fee'gă-doo)
lobster, a lagosta (lă-gohsh'tă)
lunch, o almoço (al-moh'soo)
macaroni, a massa (ma'să)
marmalade, a compota de laranja (ko*n*-po'tă dĕ lă-ra*n*'zhă)
marrow, a abóbora (ă-bo'boo-ră)
meat, a carne (karn)
melon, water melon, um melão, uma melancia (mĕ-low*n*', mĕ-la*n*-see'ă
mushrooms, os cogumelos (koh-goo-me'loosh)
mustard, a mostarda (moosh-tar'dă)
mutton, o carneiro (kăr-nay'ee-roo)
nuts, as nozes (no'zĕsh)
octopus, o polvo (pohl'voo)
olive oil, o azeite (ă-zay'eet)
olives, as azeitonas (ă-zay-toh'năsh)
omelette, uma omeleta (ohm-lay'tă)
onion, a cebola (sĕ-boh'lă)
orange, uma laranja (lă-ra*n*'zhă)
oysters, as ostras (ohsh'trăsh)
partridge, a perdiz (pĕr-deesh')
peach, um pêssego (pay'sĕ-goo)
pear, uma pera (pay'ră)
peas, as ervilhas (ĕr-vee'lyăsh)
pepper, a pimenta (pee-me*n*'tă)
pheasant, o faisão (oo fă-ee-zow*n*')
pineapple, o ananás (ă-nă-nash')
plum, uma ameixa (ă-may'ee-shă)
pork, o porco (pohr'koo); **sucking pig**, o leitão (lay-tow*n*')
potatoes, boiled, fried, as batatas, cozidas, fritas (bă-tah'tăsh, ko▪zee'dăsh, free'tăsh)
potatoes, mashed, chipped, o puré de batata, as batatas fritas (poo-r▪dĕ bă-tah'tă, bă-tah'tăsh free'tăsh)
prunes, as ameixas secas (ă-may'-shăsh say'kăsh)
pudding, o pudim (poo-dee*n*')
rabbit, o coelho (koo-ay'lyoo)
raspberries, as framboesas (fra*n*-bwe'zăsh)
rice, o arroz (ă-rohsh')
rice pudding, o arroz doce (ă-rohsh' dohs)
roasted, assado (ă-sah'doo)

roll, o pãozinho (pow-zeen-nyoo)
salad, a salada (să-lah′dă)
salt, o sal (sal)
sandwich, uma sanduíche (sand-weesh′)
sardines, as sardinhas (săr-dee′nyăsh)
sauce, o molho (moh′lyoo)
sausage, a salsicha, o chouriço (sal-see′shă, shoh-ree′soo)
shellfish, os mariscos (mă-reesh′koosh)
shrimps, os camarões (kă-mă-roynsh′)
snacks, os petiscos (pĕ-teesh′koosh)
sole, o linguado (leen-gwah′doo)
soup, a sopa (soh′pă)
spaghetti, o massa (ma′să)
spinach, o espinafre (ish-pee-na′frĕ)
squid, a lula (loo′lă)
steak, um bife (beef)
stew, o guisado (gee-zah′doo)
strawberries, os morangos (moo-ran′goosh)
sugar, o açúcar (ă-soo′kăr)
toast, as torradas (too-rah′dăsh)
tomato, o tomate (too-maht′)
tongue, a língua (leen′gwă)
trout, a truta (troo′tă)
tunny, o atum (ă-toon′)
turkey, o perú (pĕ-roo′)
vanilla, a baunilha (bow-nee′lyă)
veal, a carne de vitela (karn dĕ vee-te′lă)
vegetables, os legumes, as hortaliças (lĕ-goomsh′, ohr-tă-lee′săsh)
vegetarian diet, o regime vegetariano (re-zheem′ vĕ-zhĕ-tă-ree-ă′noo)
vinegar, o vinagre (oo vee-na′grĕ)

DRINKS

alcohol, o álcool (al′koo-ol)
beer, a cerveja (sĕr-vay′zhă)
brandy, o brandy (bran′dee)
chocolate, o chocolate (shoo-koo-laht′)
coffee, o café (kă-fe′)
coffee, black, o café (kă-fe′)
coffee, white, o café com leite (kă-fe′ kon lay′eet)
drink, uma bebida (bĕ-bee′dă)
drink, non-alcoholic, uma bebida não alcoólica (bĕ-bee′dă nown al-koo-o′lee-kă)
fruit drink, um sumo de frutas (soo′moo dĕ froo′tăsh)
gin, a genebra (zhĕ-ne′bră)
iced, fresco (fraysh′koo), com gelo (kon zhay′loo)
lemonade, uma limonada (lee-moo-nah′dă)
liqueur, um licor (lee-kohr′)
milk, o leite (lay′eet)
orangeade, uma laranjada (lă-ran-zhah′dă)

port, o vinho do Porto (vee'nyoo doo pohr'too)
rum, o rum (roon)
soda-water, a soda (so'dǎ)
spirits, os espíritos (ish-pee'ree-toosh)
tea, o chá (shah)
water, a água (a'gwǎ)
water (large bottle of), um garrafão de água (gǎ-rǎ-fown' da'gwǎ)
water (tonic-), água mineral (a'gwǎ mee-nĕ-ral')
whisky, o whisky (wees'kee)
wine, o vinho (vee'nyoo)
wine (dry), vinho seco (vee'nyoo say'koo)
wine (medium dry), vinho meio-seco (vee'nyoo may'yoo say'koo)
wine (light), vinho fraco (vee'nyoo frah'koo)
wine (red), vinho tinto (vee'nyoo teen'too)
wine (sweet), vinho doce (vee'nyoo dohs)
wine (not fully matured) vinho verde (vee'nyoo vayrd)
wine (white), vinho branco (vee'nyoo bran'koo)

Can we have lunch (dinner) here? Podemos almoçar (jantar) aqui?
poo-day'mooz al-moo-sar' (zhan-tar') ǎ-kee'

There are four of us. Somos quatro.
soh'moosh kwa'troo

When is lunch (dinner) served? A que horas é o almoço (o jantar)?
ǎ kee o'rǎz e oo al-moh'soo (oo zhan-tar')

We only want a light meal. Só queremos uma refeição leve.
so kĕ-ray'mooz oo'mǎ rĕ-fay-sown lev

We haven't much time. Não temos muito tempo.
nown tay'moosh mween'too ten'poo

Where is the dining room? Onde é a sala de jantar?
on'dee e ǎ sa'lǎ dĕ zhan-tar'

Where can we wash? Onde podemos lavar-nos?
ond poo-day'moozh lǎ-var'noosh

A table for two. Uma mesa para dois.
oo'mǎ may'zǎ pǎ'rǎ doh'eesh

A table by the window (by the wall). Uma mesa perto da janela (junto da parede).
oo'mǎ may'zǎ pair'too dǎ zha-ne'lǎ (zhoon'too dǎ pǎ-rayd')

There is a draught here. Há uma corrente de ar aqui.
ah oo'mǎ koo-rent' dar ǎ-kee'

Can we have another table? Pode arranjar-nos outra mesa?
pod ǎ-ran-zhar'nooz oh'trǎ may'zǎ

re you being served?	Está servido?
	ish-ta' sĕr-vee'doo
ay we have the menu?	A ementa, se faz favor.
	ă ee-men'tă, sĕ fash fă-vohr'
e should like ...	Queríamos ...
	kĕ-ree'ă-moosh ...
ill you bring ...	Traga ...
	trah'gă ...
hat do you recommend?	Que recomenda?
	kĕ rĕ-koo-men'dă
hat is this?	O que é isto?
	oo kee e eesh'too
hat wine do you recommend (not too expensive)?	Qual é o vinho que recomenda (não muito caro)?
	kwal e oo vee'nyoo kĕ rĕ-koo-men'dă (nown mween'too kah'roo)
o you know what this is in English?	Sabe o que é isto em inglês?
	sab oo kee e eesh'too en een-glaysh'
it good?	É bom?
	e bon
ll have that.	Quero aquilo.
	kair'oo ă-kee'loo
ell cooked, medium, underdone (*meat*)	Bem passado, não muito bem passado, mal passado.
	ben pă-sah'doo, nown mween'too ben pă-sah'doo, mal pă-sah'doo
don't want anything greasy.	Não quero coisas gordurosas.
	nown kair'oo koh'ee-zăzh goor-doo-ro'zăsh
don't like a lot of olive oil.	Não gosto de muito azeite.
	nown gosh'too dĕ mween'too ă-zay'eet
don't like garlic.	Não gosto de alho.
	nown gosh'too dal'yoo
don't like this.	Não gosto disto.
	nown gosh'too deesh'too
's too greasy (too fat).	Tem muita gordura.
	ten mween'tă goor-doo'ră
ou can take this away.	Pode levar isto.
	pod lĕ-var' eesh'too

Can I have something else?   Posso comer outra coisa?
po'soo koo-mayr' oh'trǎ koh'ee-zǎ

This is not clean.   Isto não está limpo.
eesh'too nown ish-ta' leen'poo

Bring another spoon, knife, fork.   Traga outra colher, faca, outr▪ garfo.
trah'gǎ oh'trǎ koo-lyair', fah'kǎ, oh'troo gar'foo

More bread, please.   Mais pão, se faz favor.
mǟsh pown, sě fash fǎ-vohr'

Would you like some more?   Deseja mais?
dě-zay'zhǎ mǟsh

Just a little.   Um pouco.
oon poh'koo

Would you like some other dish?   Deseja outro prato?
dě-zay'zhǎ oh'troo prah'too

Would you like anything else (something more)?   Deseja mais alguma coisa?
dě-zay'zhǎ mǟz al-goo'mǎ koh'ee-zǎ

No, thank you (I have had sufficient).   Obrigado, não desejo mais.
ob-ree-gah'doo, nown dě-zay'zhoo mǟsh

Yes, please.   Sim, faz favor.
seen, fash fǎ-vohr'

That was very good.   Estava muito bom.
ish-tah'vǎ mween'too bon

I enjoyed that.   Gostei muito.
goosh-tay'ee mween'too

We have finished.   Acabámos.
ǎ-kǎ-ba'moosh

May I have the bill, please?   Traga a conta, se faz favor.
trah'ga kon'tǎ, sě fash fǎ-vohr'

Is the service included?   O serviço está incluído?
o sěr-vee'soo ish-ta' een-kloo-ee'doo

The bill isn't correct.   A conta não está certa.
ǎ kon'tǎ nown ish-ta' sair'tǎ

Will you check it?   Pode conferi-la?
pod kon-fě-ree'lǎ

hat is this for?   A que se refere isto?
ă kě sě rě-fair' eesh'too

e didn't have that.   Não tivemos isso.
nown tee-ve'mooz ee' soo

hall pay for all of us.   Eu pago por todos.
ay'oo pah'goo poor toh'doosh

ake out separate bills.   Faça contas separadas.
fah'să kon'tăsh sě-pă-rah'dăsh

o I pay you or at the desk?   Pago aqui ou na caixa?
pah'goo ă-kee' oh nă kỹ'shă

aven't any change   Não tenho troco
nown te'nyoo troh'koo

is is for you (*i.e. tip*).   Isto é para si.
eesh'too e pă'ră see

is is for you and your col-   Isto é para si e para o seu
league (*the other waiter*).   colega.
eesh'too e pă'ră see ee pă'ră oo say'oo koo-le'gă

SHOPPING

ops are generally open from 9 a.m. to 1 p.m. and from 3 p.m. to 7 p.m.
ry day except Sunday. Newsagents and tobacconists close later. Sizes
d weights are different from those used in Britain since Portugal uses
e metric system (see p. 142).

seful shopping information for the tourist can be found regularly in the
glo-Portuguese News, which is published in Lisbon).

GENERAL SHOPPING VOCABULARY
See also under CHEMIST etc. p. 126

alarm clock, um despertador (dish-pěr-tă-dohr')
bag, um saco (sa'koo)
bathing cap, uma touca de banho (toh'kă dě bă'nyoo)
bathing costume, um fato de banho (fah'too dě bă'nyoo)
bathing trunks, os calções de banho (kal-soynzh' dě bă'nyoo)
belt, um cinto (seen'too)
beret, uma boina (boy'nă)
binoculars, os binóculos (bee-no'koo-loosh)
blouse, uma blusa (bloo'ză)
book, um livro (lee'vroo)
bow tie, um laço (lah'soo)
bra (brassiere), um soutien (soo'tee-an)

bracelet, uma pulseira (pool-say'ee-rä)
braces, suspensórios (soosh-pen-so'ree-oosh)
brooch, um broche (brosh)
brush, uma escova (ish-koh'vä)
bucket, um balde (bald)
button, um botão (boo-town')
buy, to, comprar (kon-prar')
camera, uma máquina fotográfica (ma'kee-nä foo-too-gra'fee-kä)
cap, um boné (bo-ne')
carpet, um tapete (tä-payt')
case (suit-), uma mala (ma'lä)
cash desk, a caixa (ký'shä)
china, a porcelana (poor-sě-lä'nä)
cloth, o tecido (tě-see'doo)
clothes, a roupa (roh'pä)
clothes brush, uma escova de roupa (ish-koh'vä dě roh'pä)
coat (overcoat), um sobretudo (soh-brě-too'doo)
coat-hanger, um cabide (kä-beed')
collar, o colarinho (koo-lä-ree'nyoo)
collar stud, o botão de colarinho (boo-town' dě koo-lä-ree'nyoo)
comb, um pente (pent)
cork (material), a cortiça (koor-tee'sä)
cork (stopper), uma rolha (roh'lyä)
corset, espartilho (ish-pär-tee'lyoo)
cotton, o algodão (al-goo-down')
cotton (reel of), um carro de linhas (ka'roo dě lee'nyäsh)
cotton thread, linhas de passajar (lee'nyäzh dě pä-sä-zhar')
counter, o balcão (bal-kown')
cuff links, os botões de punho (boo-toynzh' dě poo'nyoo)
department, a secção (sek-sown')
doll, uma boneca (boo-ne'kä)
drapery, as fazendas (fä-zen'däsh)
dress, um vestido (věsh-tee'doo)
dress material, os tecidos (tě-see'doosh)
dressing gown, um roupão (roh-pown')
ear-ring, um brinco (breen'koo)
elastic, o elástico (ee-lash'tee-koo)
embroidery work, os bordados (boor-dah'doosh)
envelopes, os envelopes (en-vě-lopsh')
filigree work, as filigranas (fee-lee-grä'näsh)
furniture, os móveis (mo'vaysh)
garters, as ligas (lee'gäsh)
girdle, uma cinta (seen'tä)
glass, o vidro (vee'droo)
glass (drinking), um copo (ko'poo)
glassware, os objectos de vidro (ob-zhe'toozh dě vee'droo)
gloves, (a pair of), um par de luvas (par dě loo'väsh)
gramophone record, um disco (deesh'koo)
guide book, um guia (gee'ä)
hair brush, uma escova de cabelo (ish-koh'vä dě kä-bay'loo)

handbag, uma mala de mão (ma'lă dĕ mow*n*)
handicrafts (local), os artigos regionais (ar-tee'goozh rĕ-zhee-oo-nŷsh')
handkerchief, um lenço (len'soo)
hat, um chapéu (shă-pe'oo)
headscarf, um lenço (de cabeça) (len'soo (dĕ kă-bay'să))
ink, a tinta (teen'tă)
jacket, o casaco (kă-zah'koo)
jug, um jarro (zha'roo)
jumper, um suéter (swe'tair)
lace, a renda (ren'dă)
lighter, (cigarette-), um isqueiro (ish-kay'ee-roo)
linen, o linho (lee'nyoo)
magazine, uma revista (rĕ-veesh'tă)
map, um mapa (ma'pă)
market, o mercado (mer-ca'doo)
mat (floor-) uma esteira (ish-tay'ee-ră)
material, (dress, etc.), o tecido (tĕ-see'doo)
mirror, um espelho (ish-pay'lyoo)
necklace, um colar (koo-lar')
needle, uma agulha (ă-goo'lyă)
newspaper, o jornal (zhoor-nal')
nightdress, uma camisa de dormir (kă-mee'ză dĕ đoor-meer')
nylon, o nylon (nŷ'lo*n*)
panties, as calcinhas (kal-see'nyăsh)
pants (underpants), as cuecas (koo-e'kăsh)
pen (ballpoint), uma esferográfica (ish-fe-roo-gra'fee-kă)
pen (fountain), uma caneta (kă-nay'tă)
pencil, um lápis (lahpsh)
penknife, um canivete (kă-nee-vet')
petticoat, uma combinação (ko*n*-bee-nă-sow*n*')
pins, os alfinetes (al-fee-naytsh')
pins (safety), os alfinetes de segurança (al-fee-naytsh' dĕ sĕ-goo-ra*n*'să)
pipe, um cachimbo (kă-sheen'boo)
pot, um vaso (vah'zoo)
pottery, a louçaria (loh-să-ree'ă)
present, um presente (prĕ-zent')
pullover, um pulover (poo'loh-vair)
purse (woman's), uma bolsinha (bohl-see'nyă)
purse (man's), um porta-moedas (por'tă moo-e'dăsh)
pyjamas, o pijama (pee-zhă'mă)
radio, o rádio (rah'dee-oo)
raincoat, uma gabardina (gă-băr-đee'nă)
record, um disco (deesh'koo)
record player, um gira-discos (zhee'ră deesh'koosh)
refill (for ballpoint), uma carga (kar'gă)
ribbon, uma fita (fee'tă)
ring, um anel (ă-nel')
rope, a corda (kor'dă)
rug (floor), um tapete (tă-payt')
rug (travelling), uma manta de viagem (ma*n*'tă dĕ vee-ah'zhe*n*)

sale (reduction), um saldo (sal'doo)
sale, to be on, estar à venda (ish-tar' ah ven'dă)
sandals, as sandálias (san-dah'lee-ăsh)
scarf (light), um lenço de pescoço (len'soo dě pěsh-koh'soo)
scarf (wool), um cachecol (kash-kol')
section, a secção (sek-sown')
sell, to, vender (ven-dayr')
shirt, uma camisa (kă-mee'ză)
shoes, os sapatos (să-pah'toosh)
shoe brush, uma escova de calçado (ish-koh'vă dě kal-sah'doo)
shoe laces, os atacadores de sapatos (ă-tă-kă-doh'rězh dě să-pah'toosh)
shoe polish, a pomada de sapatos (poo-mah'dă dě să-pah'toosh)
shop, a loja (lo'zhă)
shorts, os calções (kal-soynsh')
silk, a seda (say'dă)
size, a medida (mě-dee'dă)
skirt, uma saia (sÿ'ă)
slip, uma combinação (kon-bee-nă-sown')
slippers, as chinelas (shee-ne'lăsh)
soap, o sabonete (să-boo-nayt')
socks, as peugas (pee-oo'găsh)
souvenir, uma lembrança (len-bran'să)
spade (child's), uma pàzinha (pa-zee'nyă)
spectacles, os óculos (o'koo-loosh)
spectacles (case), um estojo (ish-toh'zhoo)
stockings, as meias (may'yăsh)
store, o armazém (ăr-mă-zen')
strap, uma correia (koo-ray'yă)
string, o fio (fee'oo)
suit, um fato (fa'too)
suitcase, a mala (ma'lă)
sunglasses, os óculos de sol (o'koo-loozh dě sol)
suspender belt, uma cinta (seen'tă)
suspenders, as ligas (lee'găsh)
sweets, os rebuçados (rě-boo-sah'doosh)
swimsuit, um fato de banho (fah'too dě bă'nyoo)
tablecloth, uma toalha de mesa (too-a'lyă dě may'ză)
tape recorder, um gravador (gră-vă-dohr')
textiles, os tecidos (tě-see'doosh)
tie, uma gravata (gră-vah'tă)
tiles (for decoration), os azulejos (ă-zoo-lay'zhoosh)
towel, uma toalha (too-a'lyă)
toy, um brinquedo (breen-kay'doo)
transistor (radio), um transistor (tran-zeesh-tohr')
trousers, as calças (kal'săsh)
umbrella, um guarda-chuva (gwar'dă shoo'vă)
underwear, a roupa interior (roh'pă een-tě-ree-ohr')
vest, uma camisola (kă-mee-zo'lă)
waistcoat, um colete (koo-layt')
wallet, uma carteira (kăr-tay'ee-ră)

watch, um relógio (rĕ-lo'zhee-oo)
window (shop-), a vitrina (vi-tree'nă)
wool, a lã (lan)
writing paper, o papel de carta (pă-pel' dĕ kar'tă)
zip-fastener, um fecho éclair (fay'shoo e-klair')

I must do some shopping.	Tenho de fazer umas compras.
	te'nyoo dĕ fă-zayr' oo'măsh kon'prăsh
We are going shopping.	Vamos às compras.
	vă'mooz ash kon'prăsh
I want ...	Quero ... ; (Queria ...)
	kair'oo ... ; (kĕ-ree'ă ...)
I am looking for ...	Procuro ...
	proo-koo'roo ...
We are just having a look round.	Queremos ver o que há.
	kĕ-ray'moosh vayr oo kee ah
Do you sell ... ?	Vendem ... ?
	ven'den ...
I want to buy a present (a souvenir) for ...	Queria comprar um presente (uma lembrança) para ...
	kĕ-ree'ă kon-prar' oon prĕ-zent' (oo'mă len-bran'să) pă'ră ...
Haven't you anything cheaper (anything better)?	Não tem nada mais barato (nada melhor)?
	nown ten nah'dă mỹzh bă-rah'too (nah'dă mĕ-lyor')
I want a better quality.	Quero melhor do que isto.
	kair'oo mĕ-lyor' doo kee eesh'too
I'll take this.	Levo isto.
	le'voo eesh'too
This is not what I wanted.	Não era isto que eu queria.
	nown air'ă eesh'too kee ay'oo kĕ-ree'ă
I want something bigger (smaller).	Quero uma coisa maior (mais pequena).
	kair'oo oo'mă koh-ee-za mỹ'or (mỹsh pĕ-kay'nă)
What I want is like this.	O que eu quero é assim.
	oo kee ay'oo kair'oo e ă-seen'
What size?	Que medida?
	kĕ mĕ-dee'dă
This is not my size.	Não é a minha medida.
	nowne ă mee'nyă mĕ-dee'dă

It's too big (too small). É muito grande (muito pequeno).

e mwee*n*'too gra*n*d (mwee*n*'too pĕ-kay'noo)

It's too tight (too narrow, too wide). É muito apertado (muito estreito, muito largo).

e mwee*n*'too ă-pĕr-tah'doo (mwee*n*'too ish-tray'too, mwee*n*'too lar'goo)

It's too long (too short). É muito comprido (muito curto).

e mwee*n*'too ko*n*-pree'doo (mwee*n*'too koor'too)

I don't like it. Não gosto.

now*n* gosh'too

How much is it? Quanto é?

kwa*n*'too e

I don't like the colour (the pattern). Não gosto da cor (do padrão).

now*n* gosh'too dă kohr (doo pă-drow*n*')

It is too dark (too light). É muito escuro (muito claro).

e mwee*n*'too ish-koo'roo (mwee*n*'too klar'oo)

I can't see the colour clearly. Não vejo bem a cor.

now*n* vay'zhoo be*n* ă kohr

Red, white, black. Vermelho, branco, preto.

vĕr-may'lyoo, bra*n*'koo, pray'too

Blue, light blue, dark blue. Azul, azul claro, azul escuro.

ă-zool', ă-zool' klar'oo, ă-zool' ish-koo'roo

Green, grey, brown. Verde, cinzento, castanho (marron).

vayrd, see*n*-zen'too, kăsh-tă'nyoo (ma'ro*n*)

Yellow, pink. Amarelo, cor de rosa.

ă-mă-re'loo, kohr dĕ ro'ză

I want something simple (plain). Quero uma coisa simples.

kair'oo oo'mă koh'ee-ză see*n*'plĕsh

Does this material shrink? Este tecido encolhe?

aysht tĕ-see'doo e*n*-ko'lyĕ

May I try it on? Posso experimentá-lo?

po'soo ish-pĕ-ree-men-ta'loo

May I see how it looks in the mirror? Posso ver ao espelho?

po'soo vayr ow ish-pay'lyoo

doesn't fit me very well.   Não me assenta bem.
  nown mee ă-sen'tă ben

don't care for it.   Não gosto.
  nown gosh'too

What is the charge for making   Feito por medida, quanto
one?   custa?
  fay'ee-too poor mĕ-dee'dă, kwan'too koosh'tă

When could it be ready?   Quando estará pronto?
  kwan'doo ish-tă-ra' pron'too

Not earlier?   Não pode ser mais cedo?
  nown pod sayr mỹsh say'doo

Can you send it to me?   Pode enviar-mo?
  pod en-vee-ar'moo

This is my address.   A minha direcção é esta.
  ă mee'nyă dee-re-sown' e' esh'tă

I shall take it with me.   Levo-o comigo.
  le'voo-oo koo-mee'goo

I haven't enough money with me   De momento, não tenho din-
at the moment.   heiro que chegue.
  dĕ moo-men'too, nown te'nyoo dee-nyay'ee-roo kĕ sheg

Can I pay on delivery?   Posso pagar no acto de entrega.
  po'soo pă-gar' noo a'too den-tre'gă

I shall come back for it.   Venho buscá-lo depois.
  ve'nyoo boosh-ka'loo dĕ-poh'eesh

Please keep it aside for me.   Reserve-mo, por favor.
  rĕ-zair'vĕ-moo, poor fă-vohr'

I must have it before then.   Preciso dele antes.
  prĕ-see'zoo dayl antsh

I am leaving tomorrow.   Parto amanhã.
  par'too a-mă-nyan'

Don't forget.   Não se esqueça.
  nown see ish-ke'să

Where are the toys?   Onde estão os brinquedos?
  ond ish-town' oozh breen-kay'doosh

I wanted to see some pottery   Queria ver algumas louças
(filigree-work).   (trabalhos de filigrana).
  quĕ-ree'ă vayr al-goo'măsh loh'săsh (tră-ba'lyoozh dĕ fee-lee-grä'nă)

Where can I find bracelets and so on?

Onde posso encontrar brac⟨letes e coisas desse género?

ond po'soo en-kon-trar' bra-sĕ-laytsh' ee koh'ee-zăzh days zhe'nĕ-roo

Excuse me, where can I find the stocking counter?

Faz favor, onde é a secção ⟨meias?

fash fă-vohr', on'dee e ă sek-sown' dĕ may'yăsh

Where is the (female) assistant for this section?

Onde está a empregada des⟨secção?

ond ish-tă' ă en-prĕ-gah'dă desh'tă sek-sown'

I liked a thing I saw in the window.

Gostei duma coisa que vi n⟨montra.

goosh-tay'ee doo'mă koh'ee-ză kĕ vee nă mon'tră

TOBACCONIST

VOCABULARY

box, uma caixa (kỹ'shă)
brand, a marca (mar'kă)
cigar, um charuto (shă-roo'too)
cigarette, um cigarro (see-ga'roo)
cigarette case, a cigarreira (see-gă-ray'ră)
cigarette holder, uma boquilha (boo-kee'lyă)
cigarette paper, o papel de fumar (pă-pel' dĕ foo-mar')
filter-tip (cigarette), um filtro (feel'troo)
flint, a pedra de isqueiro (pe'dră dish-kay'ee-roo)
lighter fuel, a gasolina de isqueiro (gă-zoo-lee'nă dish-kay'ee-roo)
matches, os fósforos (fosh'foo-roosh)
packet, um maço (ma'soo)
pipe, um cachimbo (kă-sheen'boo)
pipe-cleaner, o limpa-cachimbos (leen'pă kă-sheen'boosh)
tobacco, o tabaco (tă-ba'koo)
tobacconist's (shop), a tabacaria (tă-bă-kă-ree'ă)
wick, a torcida (toor-see'dă)

I want some cigarettes.

Queria uns cigarros.

kĕ-ree'ă oonsh see-ga'roosh

Where can I get cigarettes?

Onde posso comprar cigarros⟨

ond po'soo kon-prar' see-ga'roosh

Where is the nearest tobacconist's?

Onde é a tabacaria mais pró⟨ima?

on'dee e ă tă-bă-kă-ree'ă mỹsh pro'see-mă

Have you any British (American) cigarettes? | Tem cigarros ingleses (americanos)?

ten see-ga'rooz een-glay'zĕsh (ă-mĕ-ree-kă'noosh)

A packet of . . . , please. | Um maço de . . . , por favor.

oon ma'soo dĕ . . . , poor fă-vohr'

Where are these cigars from? | Donde vêm estes charutos?

don'dĕ ven ayshtsh shă-roo'toosh

How much are they? | Quanto custam?

kwan'too koosh'town

Have you a cheaper brand? | Tem uma marca mais barata?

ten oo'mă mar'kă mỹzh bă-rah'tă

I'll take these. | Levo estes.

le'voo ayshtsh

And a box of matches. | E uma caixa de fósforos.

ee oo'mă kỹ'shă dĕ fosh'foo-roosh

REPAIRS

For CAR see p. 48; for CAMERA see p. 103

I want to have these shoes repaired. | Queria estes sapatos arranjados.

kĕ-ree'ă ayshtsh să-pah'toosh ă-ran-zhah'doosh

Soles; heels (men); heels (women). | As solas; os tacões; os saltos.

ăsh so'lăsh; oosh tă-koynsh'; oosh sal'toosh

Rubber. | Borracha.

boo-ra'shă

This needs mending. | Isto precisa de conserto.

eesh'too prĕ-see'ză dĕ kon-sair'too

This is broken. | Isto partiu-se.

eesh'too păr-tee'oo-sĕ

Can you repair . . . ? | Pode consertar . . . ?

pod kon-sĕr-tar' . . .

Can you fix this? | Pode arranjar isto?

pod ă-ran-zhar' eesh'too

How long will it take? | Quanto tempo levará?

kwan'too ten'poo lĕ-vă-ra'

What will it cost? Quanto custará?
kwan'too koosh-tă-ra'

I need it (them) for tomorrow. Preciso dele (deles) para amanhã.
prĕ-see'zoo dayl (daylsh) pă'ră a-mă-nyan'

These spectacles (glasses) need repairing. Estes óculos precisam de ser arranjados.
ayshtz o'koo-loosh prĕ-see'zown dĕ sayr ă-ran-zhah'doosh

I need a new frame (lens). Preciso duma armação nova (duma lente nova).
prĕ-see'zoo doom ar-mă-sown' no'vă (doo'mă lent no'vă)

This is too tight (too loose, too slack). Isto é muito apertado (muito largo).
eesh'too e mween'too ă-pĕr-tah'doo (mween'too lar'goo)

This is not straight. Isto não está direito.
eesh'too nown ish-ta' dee-ray'ee-too

I want some dark lenses fitted on these glasses. Quero aplicar umas lentes de sol a estes óculos.
kair'oo ă-plee-kar' oo'măzh lentsh de sol ă ayshtz o'koo-loosh

My watch has stopped. O meu relógio parou.
oo may'oo rĕ-lo'zhee-oo pă-roh'

It gains (loses). Adianta (atrasa).
ă-dee-an'tă (ă-trah'ză)

Can you regulate it? Pode acertá-lo?
pod ă-sĕr-ta'loo

I need a new watch strap. Preciso de uma correia nova.
prĕ-see'zoo doo'mă koo-ray'yă no'vă

Can you stitch (sew) this? Pode coser isto?
pod koo-zayr' eesh'too

Can you darn this? Pode remendar isto?
pod re-men-dar' eesh'too

Can you mend these stockings? Pode dar uns pontos nestas meias?
pod dar oonsh pon'toosh nesh'tăzh may'yăsh

Can you have these ladders (in stockings) invisibly mended? Pode apanhar estas malhas?
pod ă-pă-nyar' esh'tăzh ma'lyăsh

Can you put a patch on this?   Pode remendar isto?

pod rĕ-men-dar' eesh'too

The lock on this case won't work.   A fechadura desta mala não funciona.

ă fĕ-shă-doo'ră desh'tă ma'lă nown foon-see-oh'nă

I need a new handle.   Preciso de uma pega nova.

prĕ-see'zoo doo'mă pe'gă no'vă

Can you shorten (lengthen) this?   Pode encurtar (pôr mais comprido) isto?

pod en-koor-tar' (pohr mỹsh kon-pree'doo) eesh'too

Can you sew a button (some buttons) on this?   Pode coser um botão (uns botões) nisto?

pod koo-zayr' ๐๐n boo-town' (oonzh boo-toynsh') neesh'too

BOOKSHOP AND STATIONER

VOCABULARY

blotting paper, o mata-borrão (ma'tă boo-rown')
book, o livro (oo leev'roo)
bookshop, a livraria (leev-ră-ree'ă)
brown paper, o papel de embrulho (pă-pel' den-broo'lyoo)
diary, um diário (dee-ah'ree-oo)
dictionary, um dicionário (dee-see-oo-nah'ree-oo)
drawing pins, os percevejos (pĕr-sĕ-vay'zhoosh)
envelopes, os envelopes (en-vĕ-lopsh')
exercise book, um caderno (kă-dair'noo)
guide book, um guia (gee'ă)
gum, a cola (ko'lă)
ink, a tinta (teen'tă)
labels, os rótulos (ro'too-loosh)
loose-leaf book, um caderno de folhas soltas (kă-dair'noo dĕ fohl'yăsh sohl'tăsh)
magazine, uma revista (rĕ-veesh'tă)
map, um mapa (ma'pa)
newspaper, um jornal (zhoor-nal')
notebook, um bloco de notas (bloh'koo dĕ no'tash), de apontamentos (dă-pon-tă-men'toosh)
paper, o papel (pă-pel')
paper clips, os clipes (kleepsh)
paste, a cola (ko'lă)
pen (ballpoint), uma esferográfica (ish-fe-roo-gra'fee-kă)
pen (fountain), uma caneta (kă-nay'tă)
pencil, um lápis (lahpsh)
pencil (propelling), uma lapiseira (lă-pee-zay'ee-ră)

pen nib, um aparo (ă-pah′roo)
phrase book, um livro de frases (leev′roo dĕ frah′zĕsh)
plan, uma planta (plan′tă)
postcards, os bilhetes postais (bee-lyaytsh′ poosh-tÿsh′)
postcards, (illustrated), os postais ilustrados (poosh-tÿz′ ee-loosh-
    trah′doosh)
refill, a carga (kar′gă)
rubber, uma borracha (boo-rah′shă)
sealing wax, o lacre (la′krĕ)
shelf, (book-), a estante (ish-tant′)
stationer's (shop), a papelaria (pă-pĕ-lă-ree′ă)
string, o fio (fee′oo)
wrapping paper, o papel de embrulho (pă-pel′ den-broo′lyoo)
writing paper, o papel de carta (pă-pel′ dĕ kar′tă)

Can you tell me where there is a Pode dizer-me onde há uma
good bookshop?   boa livraria?
    pod dee-zayr′mĕ on′dee ah oo′mă boh′ă leev-ră-ree′ă

Have you any English books Tem livros (jornais) ingleses
(papers, magazines)?   (revistas inglesas)?
    ten leev′roosh (zhoor-nÿsh′) een-glay′zăsh (rĕ-veesh′tăsh een-glay′zăsh)

Have you any books by . . . in Tem livros de . . . em inglês?
English?
    ten leev′roozh dĕ . . . en een-glaysh′

I am looking for a book by . . . Procuro um livro de . . .
    proo-koo′roo oon leev′roo dĕ . . .

The title is (it is called) . . . O título é . . .
    oo tee′too-loo e . . .

I am looking for a book on . . . Procuro um livro sobre . . .
    proo-koo′roo oon leev′roo soh′brĕ . . .

In English, if possible. Em inglês, se possível.
    en een-glaysh′, sĕ poo-see′vel

Can I order it?   Posso encomendá-lo?
    po′soo en-koo-men-da′loo

It is out of print. Está esgotado.
    ish-ta′ izh-goo-tah′doo

I can read some Portuguese, but Sei ler um pouco de português
I can't speak it well.   mas não falo muito bem.
    say′ee layr oon poh′koo dĕ poor-too-gaysh′, măzh nown fa′loo mween′too ben

Have you a book in very simple Tem um livro em portuguê
Portuguese?   muito simples?
    ten oon leev′roo en poor-too-gaysh′ mween′too seen′plĕsh

I want an English-Portuguese dictionary (and Portuguese-English).

Queria um dicionário inglês-português (e português-inglês).

kĕ-ree′ă oon dee-see-ꝏ-nah′ree-ꝏ een-glaysh′ poor-too-gaysh′ (ee poor-too-gaysh′ een-glaysh′)

I think it's on that shelf.

Parece-me que está naquela estante.

pă-res′mĕ kee ish-ta′ nă-ke′lă ish-ta*n*t′

Have you a map of the city (region, Portugal)?

Tem um mapa da cidade (da região, de Portugal)?

te*n* oon ma′pă dă see-dahd′ (dă rĕ-zhee-own′, de poor-too-gal′)

I need some (blue, black, red) ink.

Preciso de tinta (azul, preta, vermelha).

prĕ-see′zoo dĕ tee*n*′tă (ă-zool′, pray′tă, vĕr-may′lyă)

Can I have a refill for this ball-point pen?

Pode dar-me uma carga para esta esferográfica?

pod dar′mee oo′ma kar′gă pă′ră esh′tă ish-fe-roo-gra′fee-kă

I want some (large) envelopes (of this size).

Queria uns envelopes (grandes) (deste tamanho).

kĕ-ree′ă oonz e*n*-vĕ-lopsh′ (gra*n*dzh) (daysht tă-mă′nyoo)

PHOTOGRAPHY

VOCABULARY

camera, a máquina (fotográfica), (ma′kee-nă foo-too-gra′fee-kă)
colour slide, um diapositivo (dee-ă-poo-zee-tee′voo)
develop, to, revelar (rĕ-vĕ-lar′)
enlarge, to, ampliar (a*n*-plee-ar′)
enlargement, uma ampliação (a*n*-plee-ă-sow*n*′)
film, um rolo (roh′loo)
film (colour-), um rolo de cores (roh′loo dĕ koh′rĕsh)
filter, um filtro (feel′troo)
flash bulb, um 'flash' (flash)
holder, case, um estojo (ish-toh′zhoo)
knob, o botão (boo-tow*n*′)
lens, a lente (le*n*t)
light meter, o medidor de luz (mĕ-đee-dohr′ dĕ loosh)
make, a marca (mar′kă)
negative, o negativo (nĕ-gă-tee′voo)
number, o número (noo′mĕ-roo)
photograph, uma fotografia (foo-too-gră-fee′ă)
photographer, o fotógrafo (foo-to′gră-foo)

photography, a fotografia (foo-too-gră-fee'ă)
print, uma prova (pro'vă)
roll (of film), um rolo (roh'loo)
shutter, o obturador (ob-too-ră-dohr')
size, o tamanho (tă-mă'nyoo)
snap, uma foto (foh'toh)
spool, a bobina (boo-bee'nă)
strap, a correia (koo-ray'yă)
turn, to, rodar (roo-dar')
view-finder, o visor (vee-zohr')

I want some films for my camera.	Queria uns rolos para a máquina.
	kĕ-ree'ă oonzh roh'loosh prah ma'kee-nă
Have you colour films?	Tem rolos de cores?
	ten roh'loozh dĕ kohr
Size . . . ; number . . .	A medida . . . ; o número . . .
	ă mĕ-dee'dă; oo noo'mĕ-roo
Can you develop these films?	Pode revelar estes rolos?
	pod rĕ-vĕ-lar' ayshtsh roh'loosh
One print of each (_negative_).	Uma cópia de cada.
	oo'mă ko'pee-ă dĕ kă'dă
When will they be ready?	Quando estarão prontas?
	kwan'doo ish-tă-rown pron'tăsh
Will you enlarge these, please?	Pode fazer uma ampliação destas, por favor?
	pod fă-zayr' oo'mă an-plee-ă-sown' desh'tăsh, poor fă-vohr'
About this size.	Mais ou menos deste tamanho
	mўz oh may'noosh daysht tă-mă'nyoo
And what will that cost?	E quanto custará?
	ee kwan'too koosh-tă-ra'
Can you adjust (repair) this camera?	Pode arranjar (reparar) esta máquina?
	pod ă-ran-zhar' (rĕ-pă-rar') esh'tă ma'kee-nă
This doesn't work properly.	Isto não funciona bem.
	eesh'too nown foon-see-oh'nă ben
The film is jammed.	O rolo está encravado.
	oo roh'loo ish-ta' en-kră-vah'doo
The knob won't turn.	O botão não roda.
	oo boo-town' nown ro'dă

want a camera, but not an expensive one.

Quero comprar uma máquina, mas barata.

kair'oo kon-prar' oo'mã ma'kee-nã, mãzh bǎ-rah'tǎ

THE BANK AND MONEY-EXCHANGE

anks in Portugal are generally open from 10 a.m. to midday and from p.m. to 4 p.m. (Saturday 10 a.m. to midday). Money changers transact usiness usually from 9.30 a.m. to 6 p.m., and on Saturdays from 9.30 a.m. 1 p.m.

VOCABULARY

bank, o banco (ban'koo)
cash, o dinheiro (de contado) (dee-nyay'ee-roo (dě kon-tah'doo))
cash, to, sacar (sǎ-kar'), levantar (lě-van-tar')
cashier, o caixa (kỹ'shǎ)
change, to, cambiar (kan-bee-ar')
cheque, um cheque (shek)
cheque (traveller's) um cheque de viajante (shek dě vee-ǎ-zhant')
cheque book, um livro de cheques (leev'roo dě sheksh)
coin, uma moeda (moo-e'dǎ)
commission, a comissão (koo-mee-sown')
counter, o balcão (bal-kown')
exchange, o câmbio (kan'bee-oo)
form, um impresso (een-pre'soo)
letter of credit, uma carta de crédito (kar'tǎ dě kre'dee-too)
manager, o gerente (zhě-rent')
money, o dinheiro (dee-nyay'ee-roo)
money changer's, o câmbio (kan'bee-oo)
note (bank-), uma nota de banco (no'tǎ dě ban'koo)
number, o número (noo'mě-roo)
office, o escritório (ish-kree-to'ree-oo)
rate of exchange, o câmbio (kan'bee-oo)
tally (metal disc), a chapa (sha'pǎ)
section, a secção (sek-sown')
sign, to, assinar (ǎ-see-nar')
signature, a assinatura (ǎ-see-nǎ-too'rǎ)
small change, o troco (troh'koo), o dinheiro miúdo (dee-nyay'ee-roo mee-oo'doo)

xcuse me, is there a bank (a money changer's) near here?

Faz favor, há algum banco (um câmbio) próximo de aqui?

fash fǎ-vohr, ah al-goon' ban'koo (oon kan'bee-oo) pro'see-moo dǎ-kee'

Can you tell me the way to the ... Bank, please?

Podia indicar-me o caminho para o banco ..., por favor?

poo-dee'ǎ een-dee-kar'mee oo kǎ-mee'nyoo pǎ'rǎ oo ban'koo ..., poor fǎ-vohr'

When do they open (close)?   A que horas abrem (fecham)
ă kee o'răz a'bren (fay'shown)

Closed between . . . and . . .   Encerrado das . . . às . . .
en-sĕ-rah'doo dăsh . . . ash . . .

I wanted to cash some travellers'   Queria sacar (levantar) algun
cheques.   cheques de viajante.
kĕ-ree'ă să-kar' (lĕ-van-tar') al-goonsh' sheksh dĕ vee-ă-zhant'

What is the rate of exchange?   Qual é o câmbio?
kwal e oo kan'bee-oo

Can you change this money (this   Pode cambiar-me este dinheir
note) for me?   (esta nota)?
pod kan-bee-ar'mĕ aysht dee-nyay'ee-roo (esh'tă no'tă)

I have a letter of credit.   Tenho uma carta de crédito.
ten'yoo oo'mă kar'tă dĕ kre'dee-too

I want to draw . . .   Queria levantar um cheque
de . . .
kĕ-ree'ă lĕ-van-tar' oon shek dĕ . . .

Here is my passport.   Aqui está o meu passaporte.
ă-kee' ish-ta' oo may'oo pă-să-port'

What is your address?   Qual é a sua morada?
kwal e ă soo'ă moo-rah'dă

Where do I sign?   Onde devo assinar?
on'dĕ day'voo ă-see-nar'

May I speak to the cashier?   Posso falar com o caixa?
po'soo fă-lar' kon oo kỹ'shă

May I see the manager?   Posso falar com o gerente?
po'soo fă-lar' kon oo zhĕ-rent'

When shall I come back?   A que horas devo voltar?
ă kee o'răzh day'voo vohl-tar'

I can't wait until then (come   Não posso esperar até essa hor
then).   (vir a essa hora).
nown po'soo ish-pĕ-rar' ă-te' e'să o'ră (veer ă e'să o'ră)

Could you give me some small   Podia trocar-me esta nota e
change for this note?   miúdos?
poo-dee'ă troo-kar'mee esh'tă no'tă en mee-oo'doosh

I think there is an error here.   Parece-me que há aqui u
engano.
pă-res'mĕ kee ah ă-kee' oon en-ga'noo

THE POST OFFICE, LETTERS AND TELEPHONE

When telephoning, numbers should be stated individually, e.g. 84911 = oito quatro, nove, um, um; 50063 = cinco, zero, zero, seis, três. (Numbers are given on page 140).

VOCABULARY

airmail, por avião (poor ă-vee-own')
cablegram, um cabograma (kah-boo-gră'mă)
call (telephone-), uma chamada (shă-mah'dă)
collection, a tiragem (tee-rah'zhen)
counter, o guichê (gee'shay)
delivery, a entrega (en-tre'gă), a distribuição (dish-tree-bwee-sown')
dial, to, (a number), marcar um número (măr-kar' oon noo'mě-roo)
directory (telephone), a lista telefónica (leesh'tă tě-lě-fo'nee-kă)
enquiries, as informações (een-foor-mă-soynsh')
envelope, o envelope (en-vě-lop')
foreign mail, o Estrangeiro (ish-tran-zhay'ee-roo)
inland mail, Portugal (poor-too-gal')
letter, uma carta (kar'tă)
number, o número (noo'mě-roo)
operator (telephone), a telefonista (tě-lě-foo-neesh'tă)
package, um pacote (pă-kot')
parcel, a encomenda (en-koo-men'dă)
phone, o telefone (tě-lě-fon')
phone, to, telefonar (tě-lě-foo-nar')
phone box, uma cabine telefónica (kă-been' tě-lě-fo'nee-kă)
pillar box, um marco postal (mar'koo poosh-tal')
Portuguese Overseas Provinces, o Ultramar (ool-tră-mar')
post, o correio (koo-ray'yoo)
postage, a franquia (fran-kee'ă)
post-box, a caixa do correio (ky'shă doo koo-ray'yoo)
postcard, um bilhete postal (bee-lyayt' poosh-tal')
postman, o carteiro (kăr-tay'ee-roo)
post office, o correio (koo-ray'yoo)
poste restante, a posta-restante (posh'tă resh-tant')
postal order, um vale postal (val poosh-tal')
receipt, o recibo (rě-see'boo)
receiver (of phone), o auscultador (owsh-kool-tă-dohr')
register, to, registar (rě-zheesh-tar')
registered letter, uma carta registada (kar'tă-rě-zheesh-tah'dă)
reply paid, a resposta paga (rěsh-posh'tă pah'gă)
section, a secção (sek-sown')
stamp, um selo (say'loo)
telegram, um telegrama (tě-lě-gră'mă)

telegram form, o impresso de telegrama (een-pre'soo dĕ tĕ-lĕ-grä'mä)
telephone, o telefone (tĕ-lĕ-fon')
trunk call, uma chamada interurbana (shă-mah'dä een-tĕr-oor-bä'nă)

Is there a post office near here? Há um correio aqui perto?
ah oon koo-ray'yoo ă-kee' pair'too

Where is the main post office? Onde é o correio central?
on'dee e oo koo-ray'yoo sen-tral'

Which counter (section) for stamps (postal orders)? Qual é o guichê dos selos (dos vales postais)?
kwal e oo gee'shay doosh say'loosh (doozh valsh poosh-tỹsh')

I want to send this letter by air-mail. Quero enviar esta carta por avião.
kair'oo en-vee-ar' esh'tä kar'tä poor ă-vee-own'

What is the postage? Quanto é a franquia?
kwan'too e ă fran-kee'ă

What stamp do I need for this letter (this postcard)? Quanto é a franquia nesta carta (neste bilhete postal)?
kwan'too e ă fran-kee'a nesh'tä kar'tä (naysht bee-lyayt' poosh-tal')

Give me four three-escudo stamps, please. Dê-me quatro selos de três escudos, por favor.
day'mĕ kwa'troo say'loosh dĕ trayz ish-koo'doosh, poor fă-vohr'

Where is the post box? Onde é a caixa do correio?
on'dee e ă kỹ'shä doo koo-ray'yoo

I want to send this parcel. Quero enviar esta encomenda
kair'oo en-vee-ar' esh'tä en-koo-men'dä

I want to register this letter (this packet). Quero registar esta carta (este pacote).
kair'oo rĕ-zheesh-tar' esh'tä kar'tä (aysht pă-kot')

There is nothing dutiable in it. Não contém nada sujeito impostos.
nown kon-ten' nah'dä soo-zhay'ee-too ă een-posh'toosh

Do I need a special form? Preciso dum impresso especial
prĕ-see'zoo doon een-pre'soo ish-pĕ-see-al'

Where do I sign? Onde devo assinar?
ond day'voo ă-see-nar'

Don't you give me a receipt? Não me dá recibo?
nown mĕ da rĕ-see'boo

want to send a cablegram.
Quero enviar um cabograma.
kair'oo en-vee-ar' oon kah-boo-grä'mä

Where are the telegram forms?
Onde estão os impressos de telegrama?
ond ish-town' ooz een-pre'soozh dě tě-lě-grä'mä

Can you help me?
Pode ajudar-me?
pod ä-zhoo-dar'mě

Is that all right (in order)?
Está em ordem?
ish-ta' en or'den

Where is the Poste Restante?
Onde fica a posta-restante?
ond fee'kä ä posh'tä rěsh-tant'

Are there any letters (is there any mail) for me?
Há cartas (correspondência) para mim?
ah kar'täsh (koo-rish-pon-den'see-ä) pä'rä meen

My name is . . .
O meu nome é . . .
oo may'oo nohm e . . .

Here is my passport.
Aqui está o meu passaporte.
ä-kee' ish-ta' oo may'oo pa-sä-port'

My name is spelt like this . . .
O mèu nome escreve-se assim . . .
oo may'oo nohm ish-krevs' ä-seen' . . .

I am expecting a letter (a parcel) from . . .
Estou à espera duma carta (dum pacote) de . . .
ish-toh' ah ish-pair'ä doo'mä kar'tä (doon pä-kot') dě . . .

Can you forward it?
Pode despachá-la?
pod dish-pä-sha'lä

To this address.
Para este endereço.
pä'rä aysht en-dě-ray'soo

Return to sender.
Devolver ao remitente.
dě-vohl-vayr' ow rě-mee-tent'

I want to post this letter.
Quero pôr (deitar) esta carta no correio.
kair'oo pohr (day-tar') esh'tä kar'tä noo koo-ray'yoo

Would you post this for me?
Podia meter-me esta carta no correio?
poo-dee'ä mě-tayr'mee esh'tä kar'tä noo koo-ray'yoo

How much did it cost?
Quanto custou?
kwan'too koosh-toh'

What time does the (last) post go? A que horas é a (última) tiragem?
ă kee o'răz e ă (ool'tee-mă) tee-rah'zhen

When does the post come? A que horas chega o correio?
ă kee o'răsh shay'gă oo koo-ray'yoo

How many deliveries are there? Quantas distribuições há po dia?
kwan'tăzh dish-tree-bwee-soynsh' ah poor dee'ă

I want to make a phone call. Quero fazer uma chamada.
kair'oo fă-zayr' oo'mă shă-mah'dă

Have you got a telephone directory? Tem uma lista telefónica?
ten oo'mă leesh'tă tĕ-lĕ-fo'nee-kă

Can you get this number for me? Podia fazer-me uma chamad para este número?
poo-dee'ă fă-zayr'mee oo'mă shă-mah'dă pă'ră aysht noo'mĕ-roo

I don't know how your phones work. Não sei como funcionam vossos telefones.
nown say'ee koh'moo foon-see-oh'nown oozh vo'soosh tĕ-lĕ-fonsh'

What number? Que número?
ke noo'mĕ-roo

Lisbon 47735. Lisboa 47735.
leezh-boh'ă kwa'troo set set traysh seen'koo

You're through. Falem, estão ligados.
fa'len, ish-town' lee-gah'doosh

The line is engaged. A linha está interrompida.
ă lee'nyă ish-ta' een-tĕ-ron-pee'dă

The line is out of order. A linha está avariada.
ă lee'nyă ish-ta' ă-vă-ree-ah'dă

I'm sorry, there is no reply. Desculpe, não há resposta.
dish-koolp', nown ah rĕsh-posh'tă

Is that the operator? É a telefonista?
e ă tĕ-lĕ-foo-neesh'tă

You gave me the wrong number. Deu-me o número enganado
day'oo-mĕ oo noo'mĕ-roo en-gă-nah'doo

Hello! Está lá?; (Alô).
ish-ta' lah; (a-loh')

May I speak to . . . ?	Posso falar com . . . ?
	po'soo fă-lar' kon . . .
This is . . .	Aqui . . .
	ă-kee' . . .
Hold the line, please.	Não desligue, faz favor.
	nown dĕzh-leeg', fash fă-vohr'
I'll call him (her).	Vou chamá-lo (-la).
	voh shă-ma'loo ('lă)
Is that . . . ?	É . . . ?
	e . . .
Who is that? Who is speaking?	Quem fala?
	ken fa'lă
I'm sorry, I can't hear you very well.	Desculpe, mas não estou a ouvir muito bem.
	dish-koolp', măzh nown ish-toh' ă oh-veer' mween'too ben
This line is very bad.	Esta linha está muito má.
	esh'tă lee'nyă ish-ta' mween'too mah
I can't understand.	Não percebo.
	nown pĕr-say'boo
He is not in; (at home).	Não está; (em casa).
	nown ish-ta'; (en kah'ză)
May I leave a message?	Posso deixar um recado?
	po'soo day-shar' oon rĕ-kah'doo
I shall ring (phone) later.	Ligarei mais tarde.
	lee-gă-ray'ee mỹsh tard
I'll phone at one o'clock.	Telefono à uma.
	tĕ-lĕ-fo'noo ah oo'mă
Phone me about . . .	Telefone-me por volta das . . .
	tĕ-lĕ-fon'mĕ poor vol'tă dăsh . . .
Phone me at the hotel.	Telefone-me para o hotel.
	tĕ-lĕ-fon'mĕ proo oh-tel'

POLICE

Hotel and boarding house proprietors are required to fill in a form for the
police giving brief details of tourists' passports.

VOCABULARY

detective, um detective (dĕ-tek-teev')
forge, to, falsificar (fal-see-fee-kar')
forgery, uma falsificação (fal-see-fee-kă-sown')
key, a chave (shahv)
lock, a fechadura (fĕ-shă-doo'ră)
pickpocket, um carteirista (kăr-tay-reesh'tă)
police, a polícia (poo-lee'see-ă)
policeman, o polícia (poo-lee'see-ă), o guarda (gwar'dă)
police station, a esquadra (ish-kwa'dră)
report, o relatório (rĕ-lă-to'ree-oo)
robbed, roubado (roh-bah'doo)
steal, to, roubar (roh-bar')
theft, o roubo (roh'boo)
thief, o gatuno (gă-too'noo); o ladrão (lă-drown'); (*fem.* a ladra
  (la'dră)

I want to speak to a policeman. Quero falar com um polícia.
  kair'oo fă-lar' kon oon poo-lee'see-ă

Where is the police station? Onde é a esquadra?
  on'dee e ă ish-kwa'dră

Excuse me, constable (officer), Ó senhor guarda, fazia favor
  which is the way to ... ? qual é o caminho para ... ?
  o sĕ-nyohr' gwar'dă, fă-zee'ă fă-vohr', kwal e oo kă-mee'nyoo pă-ră ...

I am British. Sou inglês.
  soh een-glaysh'

I am staying at ... Estou em ...
  ish-toh' en ...

I intend staying for ... Tenciono ficar durante ...
  ten-see-oh'noo fee-kar' doo-rant' ....

I have lost my passport (my Perdi o meu passaporte (o meu
  money, my documents). dinheiro, os meus documen-
  tos).
pĕr-dee' oo may'oo pa-să-port' (oo may'oo dee-nyay'ee-roo, oozh may'oozh doo-ko-
  men'toosh)

My wallet has been stolen.	Roubaram-me a carteira. roh-bah'row*n*-mĕ ă kăr-tay'ee-ră
This case has been broken into.	Esta mala foi forçada. esh'tă ma'lă foh'ee foor-sah'dă
Somebody has broken into this room.	Este quarto foi assaltado. aysht kwar'too foh'ee ă-sal-tah'doo
We must call the police.	Temos que chamar a polícia. tay'moosh kĕ shă-mar' ă poo-lee'see-ă
I shall report this to the police.	Vou dar parte disto à polícia. voh dar part deesh'too ah poo-lee'see-ă
I reported it yesterday.	Dei ontem parte. day'ee on'ten part
Is it worth putting a notice in the papers?	Valerá a pena pôr um anúncio nos jornais? vă-lĕ-ra' ă pay'nă pohr oo*n* ă-noo*n*'see-oo noozh zhoor-nȳsh'
I shall offer a reward.	Ofereço uma recompensa. oh-fray'soo oo'mă rĕ-ko*n*-pen'să
Shall I call back tomorrow?	Volto amanhã? vǝl'too a-mă-nya*n*'

SPORTS, GAMES AND ENTERTAINMENT

VOCABULARY

SPORT

ball, a bola (bo'lă)
games, os jogos (zho'goosh)
cards, as cartas (kar'tăsh)
Football, o futebol (foot'bol)
   goal, (net), a rede (rayd)
   goal, to score a, marcar um golo (măr-kar' oo*n* goh'loo)
   ground, o campo (ka*n*'poo)
   match, o desafio (dĕ-ză-fee'oo)
   player, o jogador (zhoo-gă-dohr')
   score, o resultado (rĕ-zool-tah'doo)
Golf, o golfe (golf)
   ball, uma bola de golfe (bo'lă de golf)
   caddie, o 'caddie', o moço, (moh'soo)
   clubs (sticks), os clubes (kloobsh), os estiques (ish-teeksh')
   club (house), o clúbe (kloob)

course, o campo de golfe (kan'poo de golf)
handicap, o handicap (an'dee-kap)
hole, o buraco (boo-rah'koo)

Horse Racing, a corrida de cavalos (koo-ree'dă dĕ kă-va'loosh)
    bet, uma aposta (ă-posh'tă)
    bookmaker ('bookie'), o agenciador de apostas (ă-zhen-see-ă-doh dă-posh'tăsh)
    favourite, o favorito (fă-voo-ree'too)
    horse, o cavalo (kă-va'loo)
    jockey, o jóquei (zho'kay)
    stand, a bancada (ban-kah'dă)
    winning post, a meta (me'tă)

skates, os patins (pă-teensh')

Swimming, a natação (nă-tă-sown')
    bathe, to, tomar banho (too-mar' bă'nyoo)
    dive, to, mergulhar (mĕr-goo-lyar')
    diving-board, a prancha de saltos (pran'shă dĕ sal'toosh)
    swim, to, nadar (nă-dar')
    swimming pool, a piscina (pee-see'nă)

Tennis, o ténis (te'neesh)
    doubles, pares (pah'rĕsh)
    match, um desafio (dĕ-ză-fee'oo)
    net, a rede (rayd)
    racket, racquet, a raquete (ră-ket')
    service, o serviço, (sĕr-vee'soo)
    singles, singulares (seen-goo-lah'rĕsh)
    tennis court, o court de ténis (kohrt de te'neesh)
    table-tennis, o ping-pong (peen'pon)

Big Game Hunting, a caça grossa (ka'să gro'să)
    ammunition, as munições (moo-nee-soynsh')
    animal, o animal (ă-nee-mal')
    animal, wild (dangerous), a fera (fair'ă)
    camp, o acampamento (ă-kan-pă-men'too)
    camp, to, acampar (ă-kan-par')
    caravan, a roulotte (roo-lot'), a caravana (kă-ră-vă'nă)
    cartridges, os cartuchos (kăr-too'shoosh)
    danger, o perigo (pĕ-ree'goo)
    elephant, o elefante (ee-lĕ-fant')
    equipment, o material (mă-tĕ-ree-al')
    guide, o guia (gee'ă)
    hut, a cabana (kă-bă'nă)
    jeep, um jeep (dzheep)
    knife, a faca (fah'kă)
    lamp, uma lâmpada (lan'pă-dă)
    lion, o leão (lee-own'), [plural] leões (lee-oynsh')
    lorry, o camião (kă-mee-own')
    map, o mapa (ma'pă)
    net, uma rede (rayd)
    porter, um carregador (kă-rĕ-gă-dohr')
    reserve, a reserva de caça (rĕ-zair'vă dĕ ka'să)

rifle, a espingarda (ish-pee*n*-gar'dă)
rope, a corda (kor'dă)
stove, o fogão (foo-gown')
tent, uma tenda (te*n*'dă); uma barraca (bă-ra'kă)
torch, a lanterna eléctrica (la*n*-tair'nă ee-le' tree-kă)
track, a pista (peesh'tă)

ENTERTAINMENT

ballet, o bailado (clássico) (bў-lah'doo kla'see-koo)
ballet dancer, uma dançarina (da*n*-să-ree'nă)
box office, a bilheteira (bee-lyĕ-tay'ee-ră)
bullfight, a tourada (toh-rah'dă)
bullfighter, o toureiro (toh-ray'ee-roo)
bullring, a praça de touros (prah'să dĕ toh'roosh)
cabaret, o cabaré (kă-bă-re')
casino, o casino (kă-zee'noo)
choir, o coro (koh'roo)
cinema, o cinema (see-nay'mă)
circle (in cinema), o balcão (bal-kown')
cloakroom, o vestiário (vĕsh-tee-ah'ree-oo)
club, o clube (kloob)
concert, o concerto (ko*n*-sayr'too)
concert hall, a sala de concertos (sa'lă dĕ ko*n*-sayr'toosh)
conductor, o regente (rĕ-zhe*n*t')
dance, um baile (bўl)
dance, to, dançar (da*n*-sar')
dance hall, o salão de dança (să-lown' dĕ da*n*'să)
entertainment, a diversão (dee-vĕr-sow*n*'); [plural] diversões (dee-vĕr-soy*n*sh')
fado singer (woman), uma fadista (fă-deesh'tă)
fancy-dress ball, um baile de fantasia (bўl dĕ fa*n*-tă-zee'ă
film, um filme (feelm)
folk music (dance) group, um rancho folclórico (ra*n*'shoo fol-klo'ree-koo)
guitar, uma viola (vee-o'lă), uma guitarra (gee-ta'ră)
interval, o intervalo (ee*n*-tĕr-va'loo)
music, a música (moo'zĕe-kă)
musician, o músico (moo'zee-koo)
news reel, o documentário de notícias (doo-koo-me*n*-tah'ree-oo)
night club, uma boîte (bwat), um clube nocturno (kloob no-toor'noo)
orchestra, a orquestra (ohr-kesh'tră)
piano, o piano (pee-ă'noo)
play, to, (music), tocar (too-kar')
programme, o programa (proo-gră'mă)
radio, a rádio (rah'dee-oo)
radio (set), o rádio (rah'dee-oo)
record, um disco (deesh'koo)
record player, um gira-discos (zhee'ră deesh'koosh)
seat, um lugar (loo-gar')

screen, a tela (te'lă)
show, o espectáculo (ish-pe-ta'koo-loo)
singer, o cantor (kan-tohr'), (*fem.*) a cantora (kan-toh'ră)
song, a canção (kan-sown')
stage, o palco (pal'koo)
stalls, a plateia (plă-te'yă)
television, (TV), a televisão (tĕ-lĕ-vee-zown')
television set, o aparelho de televisão (ă-pă-ray'lyoo dĕ tĕ-lĕ-vee-zown')
theatre, o teatro (tee-ah'troo)
tune, a melodia (mĕ-loo-dee'ă)
violin, o violino (vee-oo-lee'noo)

Are there any good films on?   Há alguns filmes bons?
     ah al-goonsh' feelmsh bonsh

Where is the . . . cinema?   Onde é o cinema . . . ?
     on'dee e oo see-nay'mă . . .

When does it open?   Quando abre?
     kwan-doo a'brĕ

When does the film begin?   Quando começa o filme?
     kwan'doo koo-me'să oo feelm

When does it end?   A que horas acaba?
     ă kee o'răz ă-kah'bă

Is it in English?   É em inglês?
     e en een-glaysh'

I want to book a seat (some seats) for this afternoon (this evening, tomorrow).   Queria reservar um lugar (uns lugares) para esta tarde (esta noite, amanhã).
     kĕ-ree'ă rĕ-zĕr-var' oon loo-gar' (oonzh loo-gar'ĕsh) pă'ră esh'tă tard (esh'tă noh'eet, a-mă-nyan')

I wanted two seats in the stalls (in the circle).   Queria dois lugares na plateia (no balcão).
     kĕ-ree'ă doh'eezh loo-gar'ĕsh nă plă-te'yă (noo bal-kown')

They are too near the front (too far back).   São muito à frente (muito atrás).
     sown mween'too ah frent (mween'too ă-trash')

I want seats nearer the centre.   Queria lugares mais ao centro
     kĕ-ree'ă loo-gar'ĕsh mỹz ow sen'troo

How much is that?   Quanto é?
     kwan'too e

I can't find my seat.   Não encontro o meu lugar.
     nown en-kon'troo oo may'oo loo-gar'

How long is the interval?	Quanto tempo dura o intervalo?
	kwan'too ten'poo doo'ră oo een-tĕr-va'loo
No smoking.	É proibido fumar.
	e proo-ee-bee'doo foo-mar'
Entrance (way in); exit (way out).	Entrada; saída.
	en-trah'dă; să-ee'dă
should like to go to a dance.	Gostava de ir a um baile.
	goosh-tah'vă deer ă oon bўl
There is a dance at . . . on Saturday.	Há um baile em . . . no sábado.
	ah oon bўl en . . . noo sa'bă-doo
Should one wear evening dress?	Será necessário levar fato de cerimónia?; (for women) vestido de noite?
	sĕ-ra'nĕ-sĕ-sah'ree-oo lĕ-var' fah'too dĕ sĕ-ree-mo'nee-ă; vesh-tee'doo dĕ noh'eet
Would you care to dance?	Queria dançar?
	kĕ-ree'ă dan-sar'
May I have the honour of this dance?	Quer dar-me a honra desta dança?
	kair dar'mee ă on'ră desh'tă dansă
Can you dance the samba (waltz, tango, foxtrot)?	Sabe dançar o samba (a valsa, o tango, o foxtrot)?
	sab dan-sar' oo san'bă (ă val'să, oo tan'goo, oo foks'trot)
'm sorry, I can't dance (unfortunately).	Desculpe, não sei dançar (infelizmente).
	dish-koolp', nown say'ee dan-sar' (een-fĕ-leezh-ment')
don't dance very well.	Não danço muito bem.
	nown dan'soo mween'too ben
The band (orchestra) is very good.	A orquestra é muito boa.
	ă ohr-kesh'tră e mween'too boh'ă
What is the name of this tune?	Como se chama esta música?
	koh'moo sĕ shă'mă esh'tă moo'zee-kă
Will you have some refreshments?	Quer tomar alguma coisa?
	kair too-mar' al-goo'mă koh'ee-ză

Shall we dance again? Vamos dançar outra vez?
vă'moozh dan-sar' oh'tră vaysh

Would you like to sit down? Quer sentar-se?
kair sen-tar'sĕ

Can we meet again? Podemos encontrar-nos outra vez?
poo-day'mooz en-kon-trar'nooz oh'tră vaysh

I should like to hear some 'fados' Gostava de ouvir uns fados.
goosh-tah'vă doh-veer'oonsh fah'doosh

I should like to hear some popular music, besides 'fados'. Gostava de ouvir música popular, sem ser fados.
goosh-tah'vă doh-veer' moo'zee-kă poo-poo-lar', sen sayr fah'doosh

I should love to see some folk-dancing. Gostaria muito de ver umas danças populares.
goosh-tă-ree'ă mween'too dĕ vayr oo'măzh dan'săsh poo-poo-lah'rĕsh

I'd like to go to some popular fête. Gostava de ir a um arraial.
goosh-tah'vă deer ă oon ă-rў-al'

I should like to go to a bullfight. Gostava de ir a uma tourada.
goosh-tah'vă deer ă oo'mă toh-rah'dă

I want a seat in the shade (in the sun). Queria um lugar à sombra (ao sol).
kĕ-ree'ă oon loo-gar' ah son'bră (ow sol)

A seat in the front row (second row). Um lugar na barreira (na contra-barreira).
oon loo-gar' nă bă-ray'ee-ră (nă kon'tra bă-ray'ee-ră)

I'd like to go to a football match. Gostava de ir a um desafio de futebol.
goosh-tah'vă deer ă oon dĕ-ză-fee'oo dĕ foot'bol

I don't know how to get to the ground. Não sei como se vai para o campo.
nown say'ee koh'moo sĕ vў proo kan'poo

Two tickets for the stand. Duas bancadas.
doo'ăzh ban-kah'dăsh

Who won? Quem ganhou?
ken gă-nyoh'

The score (result) was 4-1 (2-0). O resultado foi quatro a um (dois a zero).
oo rĕ-zool-tah'doo foh'ee kwat'roo ă oon (doh'eez ă zair'oo)

The result was a draw. O resultado foi um empate.
oo rĕ-zool-tah'doo foh'ee oon en-pat'

Are you interested in sport? Os desportos interessam-lhe?
oozh dish-por'toosh een-tĕ-re'sown-lyĕ

I like watching games. Gosto de ver jogar.
gosh'too dĕ vayr zhoo-gar'

What games do you play? Que desportos pratica?
kĕ dish-por'toosh pră-tee'kă

I don't play any games. Não pratico nenhum desporto.
nown pră-tee'koo nĕ-nyoon' dish-pohr'too

I play tennis (golf). Jogo o ténis (o golfe).
zho'goo oo te'neesh (oo golf)

Is there a tennis court (golf Há um court de ténis (um cam-
course) near here? po de golfe) perto daqui?
ah oon kohrt dĕ te'neesh (oon kan'poo dĕ golf) pair'too dă-kee'

I need a tennis racquet. Preciso duma raqueta.
prĕ-see'zoo doo'mă ră-kay'tă

I need golf clubs. Preciso de clubes (estiques) de golfe.
prĕ-see'zoo dĕ kloobzh (ish-teeksh') dĕ golf

What is your handicap? Quanto dá de partido?
kwan'too da dĕ păr-tee'doo

Would you care for a game of Gostaria de jogar uma partida
...? de ...?
goosh-tă-ree'ă dĕ zhoo-gar' oo'mă păr-tee'dă dĕ ...

I should like to go riding. Queria dar uma volta a cavalo.
kĕ-ree'ă dar oo'mă vol'tă ă kă-va'loo

I should like to go fishing. Gostava de ir pescar.
goosh-tah'vă deer pĕsh-kar'

Do I need a licence? Preciso de uma licença?
prĕ-see'zoo doo'mă lee-sen'să

Can I borrow a rod? Posso arranjar uma cana em-
prestada?
po'soo ă-ran-zhar' oo'mă kă'nă en-prĕsh-tah'dă

I should like to go shooting.	Gostaria de ir caçar.
	goosh-tă-ree'ă deer kă-sar'
I need some ammunition.	Preciso de cartuchos.
	prĕ-see'zoo dĕ kăr-too'shoosh
Where can we camp?	Onde podemos acampar?
	ond poo-day'mooz ă-kan-par'
I must check my equipment.	Tenho que passar revista ao meu equipamento.
	te'nyoo kĕ pă-sar' rĕ-veesh'tă ow may'oo ee-kee-pă-men'too
Is there a radio (wireless) here?	Há rádio aqui?
	ah rah'dee-oo ă-kee'
Can you get London?	Pode apanhar Londres?
	pod ă-pă-nyar' lon-drĕsh
I wanted to hear the news.	Queria ouvir o noticiário.
	kĕ-ree'ă oh-veer' oo noo-tee-see-ah'ree-oo
I should like to hear some music.	Queria ouvir música.
	kĕ-ree'ă oh-veer' moo'zee-kă
How do you work this set?	Como se põe a trabalhar este aparelho?
	koh'moo sĕ poyn ă tră-bă-lyar' aysht ă-pă-ray'lyoo
Is this the switch for long-wave (medium-wave, short-wave)?	É este o botão das ondas compridas (médias, curtas)?
	e aysht oo boo-town' dăz on'dăsh kon-pree'dăsh (me'dee-ăsh, koor'tăsh)
Which is the volume control?	Qual é o botão de volume?
	kwal e oo boo-town' dĕ voo-loom'
The wireless is making a lot of noise.	O rádio faz muito ruído.
	oo rah'dee-oo fazh mween'too roo-ee'doo
It disturbs me at night.	Incomoda-me à noite.
	een-koo-mo'dă-mĕ ah noh'eet
Can you turn it down, please?	Pode pôr mais baixo, por favor?
	pod pohr mÿzh bÿ'shoo, poor fă-vohr'
Please turn it off.	Faz favor de desligá-lo.
	fash fă-vohr' dĕ dĕzh-lee-ga'loo

THE DOCTOR

VOCABULARY

PARTS OF THE BODY

ankle, o tornozelo (toor-noo-zay'loo)
anus, o ânus (ă'noosh)
arm, o braço (brah'soo)
back, as costas (kosh'tăsh)
blood, o sangue (sang)
body, o corpo (kohr'poo)
bone, o osso (oh'soo)
bowel, o intestino (een-tĕsh-tee'noo)
cheek, a face (fas)
chest, o peito (pay'ee-too)
chin, o queixo (kay'ee-shoo)
ear (outer), a orelha (oh-ray'lyă)
ear (inner), o ouvido (oh-vee'doo)
eyelid, a pálpebra (pal'pĕ-bră)
face, a cara (kah'ră), o rosto (rohsh'too)
finger, o dedo (day'doo)
foot, o pé (pe)
forehead, a testa (tesh'tă)
gum, a gengiva (zhen-zhee'vă)
hand, a mão (mown)
head, a cabeça (kă-bay' să)
heart, o coração (koo-ră-sown')
heel, o calcanhar (kal-kă-nyar')
hip, o quadril (kwă-dreel')
jaw, a maxila (măk-see'lă)
joint, a articulação (ăr-tee-koo-lă-sown')
kidneys, os rins (reensh)
knee, o joelho (zhoo-ay'lyoo)
knee-cap, a rótula (ro'too-lă)
leg, a perna (pair'nă)
lip, o lábio (la'bee-oo)
liver, o fígado (fee'gă-doo)
lungs, os pulmões (pool-moynsh')
mouth, a boca (boh'kă)
nail, a unha (oo'nyă)
neck, o pescoço (pĕsh-koh'soo)
neck (back of, nape of), a nuca (noo'kă)
nerve, o nervo (nayr'voo)
nose, o nariz (nă-reesh')
pulse, o pulso (pool'soo)

shoulder, o ombro (on'broo)
skin, a pele (pel)
stomach, o estômago (ish-toh'mă-goo)
throat, a garganta (găr-gan'tă)
toe, o dedo do pé (day'doo doo pe)
tongue, a língua (leen'gwă)
tonsils, as amígdalas (ă-meeg'dă-lăsh)
tooth, o dente (dent)
urine, a urina (oo-ree'nă)
wrist, o pulso (pool'soo)

GENERAL

abscess, um abcesso (ab-se'soo)
accident (traffic, road), um desastre (dĕ-zash'trĕ)
accident (at work, in home), um acidente (ă-see-dent')
allergic, alérgico (ă-lair'zhee-koo)
ambulance, uma ambulância (an-boo-lan'see-ă)
anaesthetic, um anestésico (ă-nĕsh-te'zee-koo)
appendicitis, a apendicite (ă-pen-di-seet')
appointment, uma hora marcada (o'ră măr-kah'dă)
bandage, uma ligadura (lee-gă-doo'ră)
bite, uma picada (pee-kah'dă)
bleed, to, sangrar (san-grar'), deitar sangue (day-tar' sang)
blister, uma bolha (boh'lyă)
boil, um furúnculo (foo-roon'koo-loo)
breathe, to, respirar (rĕsh-pee-rar')
bruise, uma nódoa negra (no'doo-ă ne'gră), uma contusão (kon-te zown')
burn, uma queimadura (kay-mă-doo'ră)
burn (sun-), queimadura do sol (kay-mă-doo'ră doo sol)
chill, um resfriamento (rĕsh-free-ă-men'too)
cold, uma constipação (konsh-tee-pă-sown')
constipation, a prisão de ventre (pree-zown' dĕ ven'trĕ)
consultation, uma consulta (kon-sool'tă)
convalescence, a convalescença (kon-vă-lĕ-sen'să)
convulsions, as convulsões (kon-vool-soynsh')
cough, uma tosse (tos)
cramp, a cãibra (kỹn'bră)
cure, to, curar (koo-rar')
cut, uma ferida (fĕ-ree'dă); small cut, um corte (kort)
diarrhoea, a diarreia (dee-ă-re'yă)
diet, a dieta (dee-e'tă)
doctor, o médico (me'dee-koo)
drug, um remédio (rĕ-mĕ'dee-oo)
epidemic, uma epidemia (ĕ-pi-dĕ-mee'ă)
faint, to, desmaiar (dĕzh-mỹ-ar')
fever, a febre (feb'rĕ)
fit, uma convulsão (kon-vool-sown')
flu, a gripe (greep)

fracture, uma fractura (frak-too′rǎ)
germ, um micróbio (mee-kro′bee-oo)
health, a saúde (sǎ-ood′)
hearing aid, o aparelho de ouvido (ǎ-pǎ-ray′lyoo doh-vee′doo)
hospital, o hospital (ohsh-pee-tal′)
ill, to be, estar doente (ish-tar′ doo-ent′)
illness, a doença (doo-en′sǎ)
indigestion, a indigestão (een-dee-zhĕsh-town′)
infection, a infecção (een-fe-sown′)
inflammation, a inflamação (een-flǎ-mǎ-sown′)
influenza, a gripe (greep)
injection, a injecção (een-zhe-sown′)
insect, um insecto (een-sek′too)
insomnia, a insónia (een-so′nee-ǎ)
irritation, a irritação (ee-ree-tǎ-sown′)
itching, a comichão (koo-mee-shown′)
laxative, um purgante (poor-gant′)
malaria, a malária (mǎ-lah′ree-ǎ)
medicine, o medicamento (mĕ-dee-kǎ-men′too)
nausea, a náusea (now′zee-ǎ)
nurse, a enfermeira (en-fĕr-may′ee-rǎ)
operation, a operação (oh-pĕ-rǎ-sown′)
pain, a dor (dohr)
patient, o (*fem.* a) doente (doo-ent′)
poison, o veneno (vĕ-nay′noo)
poisoning (blood-), o envenenamento de sangue (en-ve-nĕ-nǎ-men′too de sang)
rash, uma inflamação (een-flǎ-mǎ-sown′)
remedy, o remédio (rĕ-me′dee-oo)
scald, uma queimadura (kay-mǎ-doo′rǎ), uma escaldadela (ish-kal-dǎ-de′lǎ)
scar, a cicatriz (see-kǎ-treesh′)
scratch, um arranhão (ǎ-rǎ-nyown′)
sedative, um calmante (kal-mant′)
sick, to be, vomitar (voo-mee-tar′)
sick, to feel, sentir-se enjoado (sen-teer′sĕ en-zhoo-ah′doo)
sling, uma ligadura (lee-gǎ-doo′rǎ)
sore, uma úlcera (ool′sĕ-rǎ), uma infecção (een-fe-sown′)
sore throat, uma dor de garganta (dohr dĕ gǎr-gan′tǎ)
spit, to, cuspir (koosh-peer′)
splint, uma tala (tah′lǎ)
splinter, uma lasca (lash′kǎ)
spot, uma mancha (man′shǎ)
sprain, uma torcedura (toor-sĕ-doo′rǎ)
sting, uma picada (pee-kah′dǎ)
stomach-ache, a dor de estômago (dohr dish-toh′mǎ-goo)
stye, um terçol (tĕr-sol′)
sunstroke, a insolação (een-soo-lǎ-sown′)
surgeon, o cirurgião (see-roor-zhown′)
surgery, (i.e. room, office), a clínica (klee′nee-kǎ)

swell, to, inchar (een-shar')
swelling, um inchaço (een-sha'soo)
temperature, a temperatura (ten-pĕ-ră-too'ră)
test, um teste (tesht)
thermometer, o termómetro (tĕr-mo'mĕ-troo)
treatment, o tratamento (tră-tă-men'too)
urinate, to, urinar (oo-ree-nar')
vomit, to, vomitar (voo-mee-tar')
wound, uma ferida (fĕ-ree'dă)
X-ray, os raios X (rÿ'oosh sheesh)

Please call a doctor.	Faz favor de chamar um méd ico.
	fash fă-vohr' dĕ shă-mar' oon me'dee-koo
I must go to a doctor's.	Tenho de ir a um médico.
	te'nyoo deer ă oon me'dee-koo
Can you recommend a doctor?	Pode recomendar um médico
	pod rĕ-koo-men-dar' oon me'dee-koo
What are his surgery hours?	Quais são as horas de consulta
	kwÿsh sown ăz o'răzh dĕ kon-sool'tă
Can I make an appointment for . . . ?	Posso marcar consulta para . .
	po'soo măr-kar' kon-sool'tă pă'ră . . .
I don't feel well.	Não me sinto bem.
	nown mĕ seen'too ben
I have a pain (an ache) here.	Tenho uma dor aqui.
	te'nyoo oo'mă dohr ă-kee'
My wife (my son, my daughter, my husband, my father, my mother, my friend) is ill.	Minha mulher (meu filho, min ha filha, meu esposo, me pai, minha mãe, meu amig *fem.* minha amiga) está doente.
mee'nyă moo-lyair' (may'oo fee'lyoo, mee'nyă fee'lyă, may'oo ish-poh'zoo, may' pÿ, mee'nyă mÿn, may'oo ă-mee'goo, mee'nyă ă-mee'gă) ish-ta' doo-ent'	
I feel very weak.	Sinto-me muito fraco.
	seen'too-mĕ mween'too frah'koo
I feel very feverish.	Tenho muita febre.
	te'nyoo mween'tă fe'brĕ
I have a headache.	Tenho uma dor de cabeça.
	te'nyoo oo'mă dohr dĕ kă-bay'să
He has a bad (persistent) cough.	Tem muita tosse.
	ten mween'tă tos

ly nose won't stop bleeding.   O meu nariz não deixa de san-
                                               grar.
      oo may'oo nă-reesh' nown day'shă dĕ san grar'

have a sore throat (earache).   Tenho uma dor de garganta
                                          (dor de ouvido).
      te'nyoo oo'mă dohr dĕ găr-gan'tă (dohr doh-vee'doo)

looks like an infection in . . .   Parece uma infecção em . . .
      pă-res' oo'mă een-fe-sown' en . . .

have hurt my hand.   Magoei-me na mão.
      mă-gway'mĕ nă mown

am deaf (temporarily).   Estou surdo.
      ish-toh' soor'doo

erhaps the ear needs syringing.   Talvez o ouvido precise de
                                         lavagem.
      tal-vayz' oo oh-vee'doo prĕ-seez' dĕ lă-vah'zhen

ake this prescription to the   Leve esta receita para a farmá-
   chemist's.   cia.
      lev esh'tă rĕ-say'ee-tă prah făr-mah'see-ă

ake this note to the hospital.   Leve esta carta para o hospital.
      lev esh'tă kar'tă proo ohsh-pee-tal'

it serious?   É grave?
      e grahv

his is a local anaesthetic.   É um anestésico local.
      e oon ă-nĕsh-te'zee-koo loo-kal'

he effects will wear off in about   Os efeitos desaparecerão dentro
   an hour.   duma hora.
      ooz ĕ-fay'ee-toosh dĕ-ză-pă-rĕ-sĕ-rown' den'troo doo'mă o'ră

am allergic to . . .   Sou alérgico a . . .
      soh ă-lair'zhee-koo ă . . .

ow old are you?   Quantos anos tem?
      kwan'tooz ă'noosh ten

am . . .   Tenho . . . anos.
      te'nyoo . . . ă'noosh

lust I stay in bed (indoors)?   Tenho de ficar de cama (em
                                     casa)?
      te'nyoo dĕ fee-kar' dĕ kă'mă (en kah'ză)

/hat about food?   E quanto à comida?
      ee kwan'too ah koo-mee'dă

Can I eat anything?	Posso comer de tudo?
	po'soo koo-mayr' dĕ too'doo
What can I eat?	O que posso comer?
	oo kĕ po'soo koo-mayr'
You can eat what you like.	Pode comer de tudo.
	pod koo-mayr' dĕ too'doo
You mustn't eat . . .	Não deve comer . . .
	nown dev koo-mayr'
Should I come back to see you?	Devo voltar mais alguma vez?
	day'voo vohl-tar' mȳz al-goo'mă vaysh
Will you visit me tomorrow, doctor?	O senhor doutor vem ver-m amanhã?
	oo sĕ-nyohr' doh-tohr' ven vayr'mĕ ah-mă-nyan'
What is your fee, doctor?	Quanto lhe devo, doutor?
	kwan'too lyĕ day'voo, doh-tohr'

THE CHEMIST

VOCABULARY

(*For illnesses see also under* DOCTOR p. 121)

adhesive tape, o adesivo (ă-dĕ-zee'voo)
antiseptic, o antiséptico (an-tee-sep'tee-koo)
aspirin, a aspirina (ash-pee-ree'nă)
bandages, as ligaduras (lee-gă-doo'răsh)
bath salts, os sais de banho (sȳzh dĕ bă'nyoo)
bleach, (for sink, etc.) o cloreto (de cal) (kloo-ray'too dĕ kal); (for hair
  a água oxigenada (a'gwă ok-see-zhĕ-nah'dă); (for clothes) a lixívi
  (li-shee'vee-ă)
blister, a bolha (boh'lyă)
boil, um furúnculo (foo-roon'koo-loo)
bottle (medicine), o frasco (frash'koo)
brush (nail), escova de unhas (ish-koh'vă doo'nyăsh)
brush (tooth), a escova de dentes (ish-koh'vă dĕ dentsh)
chemist, o farmacêutico (făr-mă-say'oo-tee-koo)
chemist's (shop), a farmácia (făr-mah'see-ă)
comb, o pente (pent)
corn, o calo (ka'loo)
corn plaster, um emplastro (para um calo) (en-plash'troo)
cosmetics, os cosméticos (koozh-me'tee-koosh)
cotton wool, o algodão em rama (al-goo-down' en ră'mă)
cut, um corte (kort)

deodorant, o desodorizante (dĕ-zoo-doo-ree-za*nt*')
disinfectant, o desinfectante (dĕ-zee*n*-fek-ta*nt*')
drug, uma droga (dro'gă)
eye-shadow, o rimel (ree'mel)
face-cream, o creme de rosto (krem dĕ rohsh'too)
face-powder, o pó de arroz (po dă-rohsh')
fruit salts, os sais de fruta (sÿzh dĕ froo'tă)
gargle, o gargarejo (găr-gă-ray'zhoo)
hair, o cabelo (kă-bay'loo)
hair cream, o creme para o cabelo (krem pă'ră oo kă-bay'loo)
hair curlers, os rolos de cabelo (roh'loozh dĕ kă-bay'loo)
hair grip, um gancho (ga*n*'shoo)
hair lacquer, a laca (la'kă)
hair lotion, a loção (para o cabelo) (loo-sow*n*')
hair oil, a brilhantina (bree-lya*n*-tee'nă)
hairpins, os ganchos (ga*n*'shoosh)
hair slide, um gancho (ga*n*'shoo)
inhaler, o inalador (ee-nă-lă-dohr')
insecticide, uma insecticida (ee*n*-sek-tee-see'dă)
jar (of face-cream, etc.), o boião (boh-yow*n*')
laxative, o laxativo (lak-să-tee'voo)
lint, a gaze (gahz)
lipstick, o bâton (ba'to*n*)
lotion, uma loção (loo-sow*n*')
make-up, a maquilhagem (mă-kee-lyah'zhe*n*)
medicine, o medicamento (mĕ-dee-kă-me*n*'too)
mirror, o espelho (ish-pay'lyoo)
nail, a unha (oo'nyă)
nail file, a lima de unhas (lee'mă doo'nyăsh)
nail varnish, o verniz das unhas (vĕr-neezh' dăz oo'nyăsh)
nail-varnish remover, a acetona (ă-sĕ-toh'nă)
ointment, a pomada (poo-mah'dă)
paper handkerchiefs, os lenços de papel (le*n*'soozh dĕ pă-pel')
pastilles (throat-), as pastilhas para a garganta (păsh-tee'lyăsh prah
    găr-ga*n*'tă)
perfume, o perfume (pĕr-foom')
pills, os comprimidos (ko*n*-pri-mee'doosh)
plaster, o adesivo (ă-dee-zee'voo)
powder (face), o pó de arroz (po dă-rohsh')
prescription, a receita (rĕ-say'ee-tă)
pumice stone, uma pedra-pomes (pe'dră pomsh)
quinine, o quinino (ki-nee'noo)
razor (safety-), a gilete (zhee-layt')
razor blade, a lâmina (de barba) (lă'mee-nă dĕ bar'bă)
rouge, o rouge (roozh)
sanitary towels, os pensos higiénicos (pe*n*'sooz ee-zhee-e'nee-koosh)
scissors, a tesoura (tĕ-zoh'ră)
shaving brush, o pincel de barba (pee*n*-sel' dĕ bar'bă)
shaving cream, o creme de barbear (krem dĕ băr-bee-ar')
shaving soap, o sabão de barba (să-bow*n*' dĕ bar'bă)

sleeping tablets, os sedativos (sĕ-dă-tee'voosh)
soap, o sabonete (să-boo-nayt')
sponge, a esponja (ish-po*n*'zhă)
stomach powder, os pós digestivos (pozh dee-zhĕsh-tee'voosh)
sunburn lotion, a loção contra as queimaduras (loo-sow*n*' ko*n*'tră ăsh
    kay-mă-door'răsh)
sunglasses, os óculos de sol (o'koo-loozh dĕ sol)
sun-tan cream, o creme para brónzear (krem pă'ră bro*n*-zee-ar')
sun-tan lotion, óleo para bronzear (o'lee-oo pă'ră bro*n*-zee-ar')
tablet, um comprimido (ko*n*-pri-mee'doo)
talcum powder, o pó de talco (po dĕ tal'koo)
toilet paper, o papel higiénico (pă-pel' ee-zhee-e'nee-koo)
toothbrush, a escova de dentes (ish-koh'vă dĕ de*n*tsh)
toothpaste, a pasta de dentes (pash'tă dĕ de*n*tsh)
tooth powder, os pós dentifricos (pozh de*n*-tee'free-koosh)
tube (of ointment, etc.), a bisnaga (beezh-nah'gă)

Excuse me, I am looking for a chemist's. Fazia favor, ando à procura duma farmácia.
fă-zee'ă fă-vohr', a*n*'doo ah proo-koo'ră doo'mă făr-mah'see-ă

Is there a chemist near here? Há uma farmácia perto daqui?
ah oo'mă făr-mah'see-ă pair'too dă-kee'

Can you give me something for this? Pode dar-me alguma coisa para isto?
pod dar'mĕ al-goo'mă koh'ee-ză pă'ră eesh'too

Can you make up this prescription for me, please? Pode aviar-me esta receita, po favor?
pod ă-vee-ar'mĕ esh'tă rĕ-say'ee-tă, poor fă-vohr'

I got the prescription in England. Arranjei a receita em Inglaterra
ă-ra*n*-zhay'ee ă rĕ-say'ee-tă e*n* een-glă-te'ră

When will it be ready? Quando estará pronta?
kwa*n*'doo ish-tă-ra' pro*n*'ta

Can you send it to . . . ? Podia mandá-lo a . . . ?
poo-dee'ă ma*n*-da'loo ă . . .

Can you give me something for . . . ? Pode dar-me qualquer coisa para . . . ?
pod dar'mĕ kwal'kair koh'ee-ză pă'ră . . .

A chill, cold, cough, headache, sunburn. Um resfriamento, uma cons tipação, uma tosse, uma do de cabeça, a queimadura d sol.
oo*n* rĕsh-free-ă-me*n*'too, oo'mă ko*n*sh-tee-pă-sow*n*', oo'mă tos, oo'mă dohr d
kă-bay'să, ă kay-mă-doo'ră doo sol

Constipation, indigestion, diarrhoea, insect bites, a sore
throat.
A prisão de ventre, a indigestão,
a diarreia, picadas de insec-
tos, a dor de garganta.

ă pree-zown' dĕ ven'trĕ, ă een-dee-zhĕsh-town', ă dee-ă-re'yă, pee-kah'dăzh deen-sek'
toosh, ă dohr dĕ găr-gan'tă

I have been stung by a wasp (a
bee, a mosquito).
Fui mordido por uma vespa
(uma abelha, um mosquito).

foo'ee moor-dee'doo poor oo'mă vaysh'pa (oom ă-bay'lyă, oon moosh-kee'too)

I have something in my eye.
Tenho qualquer coisa na vista.

te'nyoo kwal'kair koh'ee-ză nă veesh'tă

I feel sick, feverish.
Sinto-me enjoado, com febre.

seen'too-mĕ en-zhoo-ah'doo, kon fe'brĕ

I feel faint, giddy.
Sinto-me fraco, com tonturas.

seen'too-me frah'koo, kon ton-too'răsh

I don't feel well.
Não me sinto bem.

nown mĕ seen'too ben

Can I speak to you privately?
Posso falar-lhe em particular?

po'soo fă-lar'lyĕ en păr-tee-koo-lar'

May I speak to a (female) assistant, (male) assistant?
Posso falar com uma empregada, (um empregado)?

po'soo fă-lar' kon oo'mă en-prĕ-gah'dă (oon en-prĕ-gah'doo)

I am waiting to speak to that
lady (that gentleman).
Queria falar com aquela senhora (aquele senhor).

kĕ-ree'ă fă-lar' kon ă-ke'lă sĕ-nyoh'ră (ă-kayl' sĕ-nyohr')

I am being served.
Já estou atendido.

zhah ish-toh' ă-ten-dee'doo

Can you recommend a doctor?
Pode recomendar-me um médico?

pod rĕ-koo-men-dar'mĕ oon me'dee-koo

Can you call a taxi?
Podia chamar um táxi?

poo-dee'ă sha-mar' oon tak'see

Directions for use.
O modo de usar.

oo mo'doo doo-zar'

For external use only.
Só para uso externo.

so pă'ră oo'zoo ish-tair'noo

Poison.
Veneno.

vĕ-nay'noo

Dangerous.
Perigoso.

pĕ-ree-goh'zoo

One teaspoonful (tablespoonful) in a glass of water.	Uma colher de chá (uma colher de sopa) num copo de água.

oo'mă koo-lyair' dě shah (oo'mă koo-lyair' dě soh'pă) noon ko'poo dag'wă

Take . . . three times a day (every four hours) before (after) meals.	Tome . . . três vezes ao dia (de 4 em 4 horas) antes (depois) das refeições.

tom . . . trayzh vay'zěsh ow dee'ă (dě kwa'troo en kwa'troo o'răsh) antsh (dě-poh'eezh) dăzh rě-fay-soynsh'

THE DENTIST

VOCABULARY

appointment, uma consulta (kon-sool'tă)
decay, a cárie (kah'ree-ě)
dentist, o dentista (den-teesh'tă)
denture, a dentadura (den-tă-doo'ră)
drill, a broca (bro'kă)
extract, to, tirar (tee-rar')
extraction, a extracção (ish-trah-sown')
fill, to (tooth), chumbar (shoon-bar'), obturar (ob-too-rar')
filling (ordinary), uma obturação (ob-too-ră-sown')
filling (gold), uma obturação em ouro (ob-too-ră-sown' en oh'roo)
gas, o gás (gash)
gum, a gengiva (zhen-zhee'vă)
injection, uma injecção (een-zhe-sown')
jaw, o queixo (kay'ee-shoo)
nerve, o nervo (nayr'voo)
pain, a dor (dohr)
plate (dental), a placa dentária (pla'kă den-tah'ree-ă)
rinse out, to, lavar (lă-var')
teeth, os dentes (dentsh)
teeth (false), os dentes postiços (dentsh poosh-tee'soosh)
tooth, um dente (dent)
toothache, a dor de dentes (dohr de dentsh)

I want to go to a dentist.	Quero ir a um dentista.

kair'oo eer ă oon den-teesh'tă

I have got toothache.	Tenho dor de dentes.

te'nyoo dohr dě dentsh

I have lost a filling.	Perdi uma obturação (um chumbo).

pěr-dee' oo'mă ob-too-ră-sown' (oon shoon'boo)

I have a broken tooth.   Tenho um dente partido.
te'nyoo oon dent păr-tee'doo

I can't see any signs of decay.   Não vejo sinais de cárie.
nown vay'zhoo see-nỹzh' dě kah'ree-ĕ

Must it come out?   É preciso tirá-lo?
e prĕ-see'zoo tee-ra'loo

That hurts.   Isso dói.
ee'soo doy

Can I have a (temporary) filling?   Podia fazer-me uma obturação (provisória)?
poo-dee'ă fă-zayr'mě oo'mă ob-too-ră-sown' (proo-vee-zo'ree-ă)

I have a broken denture.   A minha dentadura está partida.
ă mee'nyă den-tă-doo'ră ish-ta' păr-tee'dă

How long will it take?   Quanto tempo levará?
kwan'too ten'poo lĕ-vă-ra'

I leave on . . .   Parto . . .
par'too . . .

The gum is sore.   A gengiva está dorida.
ă zhen-zhee'vă ish-ta' doo-ree'dă

It is bleeding.   Está a sangrar.
ish-ta' ă san-grar'

That is much better.   Isso é muito melhor.
ee'soo e mween'too mĕ-lyor'

How much do I owe you?   Quanto lhe devo, doutor?
kwan'too lyĕ day'voo, doh-tohr'

THE HAIRDRESSER

VOCABULARY

bleach, to (hair), oxigenar (ok-see-zhĕ-nar')
brush, uma escova (ish-koh'vă)
brush, to, escovar (ish-koo-var')
clippers, a máquina (ma'kee-nă)
comb, um pente (pent)
comb, to, pentear (pen-tee-ar')
cut, to, cortar (koor-tar')
dryer, o secador (sĕ-kă-dohr')
face massage, uma massagem à cara (mă-sah'zhen ah kah'ră)

hair, o cabelo (kă-bay'loo)
hairdresser (men's), o barbeiro (băr-bay'ee-roo)
hairdresser (ladies'), o cabeleireiro (kă-bĕ-lay-ray'ee-roo)
hair style (men), o corte (kort)
hair style (women), o penteado (pen-tee-ah'doo)
manicure, uma manicure (mă-nee-koor')
manicurist, a manicura (mă-nee-koo'ră)
nails, as unhas (oo'nyăsh)
perfume, o perfume (pĕr-foom')
perm (permanent wave), uma permanente (pĕr-mă-nent')
razor, a navalha (nă-va'lyă)
set, uma mise (meez)
shampoo, um shampoo (shan-poo')
shave, to, fazer a barba (fă-zayr' ă bar'bă)
trim, to, aparar (ă-pă-rar')

Can I make an appointment?	Posso marcar uma hora? po'soo măr-kar' oo'mă o'ră
When can I come?	Quando posso vir? kwan'doo po'soo veer
I want a haircut.	Quero cortar o cabelo. kair'oo koor-tar' oo kă-bay'loo
I want a trim.	Quero aparar a cabelo. kair'oo ă-pă-rar' oo kă-bay'loo
Not too short.	Não muito curto. nown mween'too koor'too
Fairly short.	Bastante curto. bash-tant' koor'too
At the back and sides.	Atrás e dos lados. ă-trazh' ee doozh lah'doosh
Don't take a lot off the top.	Não corte muito por cima. nown kort mween'too poor see'mă
Don't use the razor on the neck.	Não use a navalha no pescoço. nown ooz ă nă-va'lyă noo pĕsh-koh'soo
I part my hair on this side.	Faço o risco deste lado. fah'soo oo reesh'koo daysht lah'doo
I comb my hair straight back.	Penteio-me para trás. pen-tay'oo-mĕ pă'ră trash
Don't put anything on.	Não ponha nada. nown poh'nyă nah'dă

little spray; a little cream.
Só um borrifo; um pouco de creme.
so oon boo-ree'foo; oon poh'koo de krem

want a shave.
Quero fazer a barba.
kair'oo fă-zayr' ă bar'bă

should like a shampoo.
Queria um shampoo.
kĕ-ree'ă oon shan-poo'

want a shampoo and set.
Quero um shampoo e uma mise.
kair'oo oon shan-poo' e oo'mă meez

want my hair washed.
Quero uma lavagem ao cabelo.
kair'oo oo'mă lă-vah'zhen ow kă-bay'loo

The water is too hot (too cold).
A água está muito quente (muito fria).
a'gwă ish-ta' mween'too kent (mween'too free'ă)

want a permanent wave.
Quero uma permanente.
kair'oo oo'mă pĕr-mă-nent'

want a colour rinse.
Quero uma ransagem.
kair'oo oo'mă ran-sah'zhen

My hair is dry now.
O meu cabelo está seco agora.
oo may'oo kă-bay'loo ish-ta' say'koo ă-go'ră

The dryer is too hot.
O secador está muito quente.
oo sĕ-kă-dohr' ish-ta' mween'too kent

Can I have my nails manicured?
Posso tratar as unhas?
po'soo tră-tar' ăz oo'nyăsh

SOME PUBLIC NOTICES

Aberto
Open
ă-bair'too

Agência de viagens
Travel agency
ă-zhen'see-ă dĕ vee-ah'zhensh

Água potável
Drinking water
a'gwă poo-tah'vel

Alfândega
Customs
al-fan'dĕ-gă

Aluga-se
For hire, to let
ă-loo'gă-sĕ

Assinatura	Signature
	ă-see-nă-too′ră
Autocarro	Bus
	ow-too-ka′roo
Bater	Knock
	bă-tayr′
Bilheteira	Booking office
	beel-yĕ-tay′ee-ră
Bombeiros	Fire Brigade
	bon-bay′ee-roosh
Carregar	Press
	kă-rĕ-gar′
Consulado	Consulate
	kon-soo-lah′doo
Conto	1,000 escudos
	kon′too
Correio	Post Office
	koo-ray′yoo
Embaixada	Embassy
	en-bȳ-shah′dă
Empurrar	Push
	en-poo-rar′
Encerrado	Closed
	en-sĕ-rah′doo
Entrada	Entrance
	en-trah′dă
Entrada livre	Admission free
	en-trah′dă leev′rĕ
Endereço	Address
	en-dĕ-ray′soo
Fechado	Closed
	fĕ-shah′doo
Foguete	Express (train)
	foo-gayt′
Frio	Cold
	free′oo
Homens	Gentlemen (lavatory)
	o′mensh

Informações   Enquiries
een-foor-mă-soynsh'

Leilão   Auction
lay-lown'

Livre   Free, vacant
leev'rĕ

Lotação esgotada   House full (cinema)
loo-tă-sown' izh-goo-tah'dă

Morada   Address, residence
moo-rah'dă

Não se debruçar   Do not lean out
nown sĕ dĕ-broo-sar'

Nome   Name
nohm

Pensão, Pensão completa   Boarding house, Full board
pen-sown', pen-sown' kon-ple'tă

Perigo   Danger
pĕ-ree'goo

Proibido   Forbidden
proo-ee-bee'doo

Puxar   Pull
poo-shar'

Rápido   Express
ra'pee-doo

Retrete   Lavatory
rĕ-trayt'

Saída   Exit
să-ee'dă

Saldo   Sale
sal'doo

Senhoras   Ladies (lavatory)
sĕ-nyoh'răsh

Tocar   Ring
too-kar'

Trabalhos   Repairs (roads, bridges, etc.)
tră-ba'lyoosh

Veneno   Poison
vĕ-nay'noo

ROAD SIGNS

Curva perigosa.   Dangerous bend.
koor'vă pĕ-ree-go'ză

Descida íngreme.   Steep hill.
dĕsh-see'dă een'grĕm

Desvio   Diversion, detour.
dĕzh-vee'oo

Encruzilhada.   Crossroads.
en-kroo-zee-lyah'dă

Estacionamento proibido.   No parking.
ish-tă-see-oo-nă-men'too proo-ee-bee'doo

Guiar com cuidado.   Drive with care.
gee-ar' kon kwee-dah'doo

Parar.   Stop.
pă-rar'

Passagem de nível.   Level crossing.
pă-sah'zhen dĕ nee'vel

Perigo.   Danger.
pĕ-ree'goo

Posto de socorros.   First-aid post.
ohsh'too dĕ soo-koh'roosh

Proibido entrar.   No entrance.
proo-ee-bee'doo en-trar'

Seguir pela direita, esquerda.   Keep right, left.
sĕ-geer' pĕ'lă dee-ray'ee-tă, ish-kayr'dă

Sentido proibido.   No through road.
sen-tee'doo proo-ee-bee'doo

Sentido único.   One-way street.
sen-tee'doo oo'nee-koo

Trabalhos.   Road works.
tră-ba'lyoosh

Trânsito vedado.   Road closed.
tran'zee-too vĕ-dah'doo

Velocidade máxima.   Maximum speed.
vĕ-loo-see-dahd' ma'see-mă

PORTUGUESE ABBREVIATIONS

A.C.P. (*Automóvel Clube de Portugal*) Portuguese Automobile Club

Av. (*Avenida*) Avenue

Cª, Cⁱᵃ. (*Companhia*) Company

C.P. (*Caminhos de Ferro da Companhia Portuguesa*) Portuguese State Railways

D. (*Dom, Dona*) Mr., Mrs., Miss (with Christian names only)

De 2ª. (*de segunda classe*) 2nd class (hotels, boarding houses)

D., Dᵗᵒ. (*direito*) On the right (in addresses of flats)

End. Teleg. (*endereço telegráfico*) Telegram address

Esc. (*escudo*) Escudo

E., Esq. (*esquerdo*) On the left (in addresses of flats)

H.P. Horse-power

Idem. Ditto

Kg. (*quilograma*) Kilogram

Km. (*quilómetro*) Kilometre

Lda. (*limitada*) Ltd.

M. (*metro*) Metre

Nª Sʳᵃ. (*Nossa Senhora*) Our Lady

P. (*praça*) Square

P.I.D.E. (*Polícia internacional e de defesa do estado*) Security Police

R. (*rua*) Street

R/C (*rés-do-chão*) Ground floor

S., Sᵗᵒ, Sᵗᵃ. (*são, santo, santa*) Saint

Soc. (*sociedade*) Society (commerce)

Sʳ. (*senhor*) Mr.

Sʳᵃ. (*senhora*) Mrs., Miss

TAP (*Transportes Aéreos Portugueses*) Portuguese Airways

1º (andar) (*primeiro* (*andar*)) First floor

2º (andar) (*segundo* (*andar*)) Second floor

COUNTRIES, NATIONALITIES AND PLACE NAMES

The Portuguese usually use 'England' and 'the English' as equivalents of 'Britain' and 'the British'. 'Americano' is nowadays the normal term for a citizen of the USA.

Africa	**África.** a'free-kă
America, American.	**América, americano.** ă-me'ree-kă, ă-mĕ-ree-kă'noo
Angola.	**Angola.** an-go'lă
Azores.	**Os Açores.** ooz ă-soh'rĕsh
Brazil, Brazilian.	**O Brasil, brasileiro.** o bră-zeel', bră-zee-lay'ee-roo
British.	**Britânico.** bree-tă'nee-koo
Canada, Canadian.	**O Canadá, canàdiano.** oo kă-nă-da', kă-nă-dee-ă'noo
Cape Verde.	**Cabo Verde.** kah'bo vayrd
England, English.	**Inglaterra, inglês.** een-glă-te'ră, een-glaysh'
France, French.	**França, francês.** fran'să, fran-saysh'
Germany, German.	**Alemanha, alemão.** ă-lĕ-mă'nyă, ă-lĕ-mown'
Great Britain.	**Grã-Bretanha.** gran brĕ-ta'nyă
Ireland, Irish.	**Irlanda, irlandês.** eer-lan'dă, eer-lan-daysh'
Madeira.	**Madeira.** mă-day'ee-ră
Mozambique.	**Moçambique.** moo-san-beek'

Portugal, Portuguese.   Portugal, português.
      poor-too-gal', poor-too-gaysh'

Rhodesia, Rhodesian.   A Rodésia, rodesiano.
     ă roo-de'zee-ă, roo-dě-zee-ă'noo

Scotland, Scottish.   Escócia, escocês.
     ish-ko'see-ă, ish-koo-saysh'

South Africa, South African.   A África do Sul, sulafricano.
     a'free-kă do sool, sool-ă-free-kă'noo

Spain, Spanish.   Espanha, espanhol.
     ish-pă'nya, ish-pă-nyol'

U.S.A.   Os Estados Unidos.
     ooz ish-tah'dooz oo-nee'doosh

Wales, Welsh.   O País de Gales, galês.
     oo pă-eezh' dě galsh, gă-laysh'

PLACE NAMES

Alcobaça
al-koo-bah'să

(O) Algarve
oo al-garv'

(O) Alentejo
oo a-len-te'zhoo

Arrábida
ă-ra'bee-dă

Aveiro
ă-vay'ee-roo

Batalha
bă-ta'lyă

(A) Beira
ă bay'ee-ră

Braga
brah'gă

Bragança
bră-gan'să

Buçaco (Bussaco)
boo-sah'koo

Cascais
kash-kỹsh'

Coimbra
koo-een'bră

Covilhã
koo-veel-yan'

(O) Douro
oo doh'roo

Estoril
ish-too-reel'

Évora
e'voo-ră

Faro
fah'roo

Figueira da Foz
fee-gay'ee-ră dă fosh

Funchal
foon-shal'

Guimarães
gee-mă-rỹnsh'

Lagos
lah'goosh

Leixões
lay-shoy*n*sh'

Lisboa (Lisbon)
leezh-boh'ă

Nazaré
nă-ză-re'

(O) Porto (Oporto)
oo pohr'too

(O) Minho
oo mee'nyoo

(O) Mondego
oo mo*n*-day'goo

Olhão
oh-lyow*n'*

Peniche
pĕ-neesh'

Praia da Rocha
prў'ă dă ro'shă

Queluz
kĕ-loosh'

Sagres
sa'grĕsh

Santarém
san-tă-ren'

Sesimbra
sĕ-zeen'bră

Setúbal
sĕ-too'bal

Sintra (Cintra)
see*n*'tră

(O) Tejo (The Tagus)
(oo) te'zhoo

Trás-os-Montes
traz-oozh-mo*n*tsh'

Vila Franca de Xira
vee'lă fra*n*'kă dĕ shee'ră

Viseu
vee-zay'oo

NUMBERS

0 = Zero (zair'oo)
1 = Um; uma (*before feminine noun*) (oo*n*; oo'mă)
2 = Dois; duas (*before feminine nouns*) (doh'eesh; đoo'ăsh)
3 = Três (traysh)
4 = Quatro (kwa'troo)
5 = Cinco (see*n*'koo)
6 = Seis (say'eesh)
7 = Sete (set)
8 = Oito (oh'ee-too)
9 = Nove (nov)
10 = Dez (desh)
11 = Onze (o*n*z)
12 = Doze (dohz)
13 = Treze (tray'zĕ)
14 = Catorze (kă-tohrz')
15 = Quinze (kee*n*z)
16 = Dezasseis (dĕ-ză-say'eesh)
17 = Dezassete (dĕ-ză-set')
18 = Dezoito (de-zoh'ee-too)

19 = Dezanove (dĕ-ză-nov′)
20 = Vinte (veent)
21 = Vinte e um (veent-ee-oon′)
22 = Vinte e dois (veent-ee-doh′eesh)
30 = Trinta (treen′tă)
40 = Quarenta (kwă-ren′tă)
50 = Cinquenta (seen-kwen′tă)
60 = Sessenta (sĕ-sen′tă)
70 = Setenta (sĕ-ten′tă)
80 = Oitenta (oy-ten′tă)
90 = Noventa (noo-ven′tă)
100 = Cem (sen)
101 = Cento e um (sen′too ee oon)
102 = Cento e dois (sen′too ee doh′eesh)
200 = Duzentos (doo-zen′toosh)
300 = Trezentos (trĕ-zen′toosh)
400 = Quatrocentos (kwa′troo-sen′toosh
500 = Quinhentos (keen-yen′toosh)
600 = Seiscentos (saysh-sen′toosh)
700 = Setecentos (set-sen′toosh)
800 = Oitocentos (oy-too-sen′toosh)
900 = Novecentos (nov-sen′toosh)
1,000 = Mil (meel)
2,000 = Dois mil (doh′eezh meel)
a million, Um milhão (oon mee-lyown′)
per cent. = por cento (poor sen′too)

first = primeiro (pri-may′ee-roo)
second = segundo (sĕ-goon′doo)
third = terceiro (tĕr-say′ee-roo)
fourth = quarto (kwar′too)
fifth = quinto (keen′too)
sixth = sexto (saysh′too)
a half = a metade (ă mee-tahd′)
a third = a terça parte (ă tayr′să part)
a quarter = a quarta parte (ă kwar′tă part)
two thirds = dois terços (doh′eesh tayr′soosh)

Note: "Tres (3) and "Treze"(13) may be confused when they stand immedi-
ately before a vowel (e.g. três escudos; treze escudos). "Treze" is, therefore,
often pronounced "tray′zee" for the sake of clarity).

WEIGHTS AND MEASURES

The metric system is used in Portugal. The following tables give approximate equivalents:

WEIGHT

100 gramas	=	$3\frac{1}{2}$ oz.
1 quilograma	=	2 lb. 3 oz.

CAPACITY

1 litro	=	$1\frac{3}{4}$ pints
$4\frac{1}{2}$ litros	=	1 gallon

LENGTH

1 centímetro	=	$\frac{3}{8}$ inch
$2\frac{1}{2}$ centímetros	=	1 inch
30 centímetros	=	1 foot
91 centímetros	=	1 yard
1 metro	=	39 inches
1 quilómetro	=	0.62 mile
1.6 quilómetros	=	1 mile

TEMPERATURE

To convert degrees Centigrade into degrees Fahrenheit, multiply by $\frac{9}{5}$ and add 32. Thus, $20°$ C. $= 68°$ F. $(20 \times \frac{9}{5} + 32 = 68)$.

TYRES

Tyre pressures are measured on the U.K. standard.

CLOTHING SIZES

DRESSES AND SUITS (Women)

British	36	38	40	42	44	46
American	34	36	38	40	42	44
Continental	42	44	46	48	50	52

DRESSES AND SUITS (Junior Miss)

British	32	33	35	36	38	39
American	10	12	14	16	18	20
Continental	38	40	42	44	46	48

MEN'S SUITS AND OVERCOATS

British and American	36	38	40	42	44	46
Continental	46	48	50	52	54	56

SHIRTS

British and American	14	$14\frac{1}{2}$	15	$15\frac{1}{2}$	16	$16\frac{1}{2}$	17
Continental	36	37	38	39	41	42	43

SOCKS

British and American	$9\frac{1}{2}$	10	$10\frac{1}{2}$	11	$11\frac{1}{2}$
Continental	38–39	39–40	40–41	41–42	42–43

HATS

British and American	$6\frac{1}{2}$	$6\frac{5}{8}$	$6\frac{3}{4}$	$6\frac{7}{8}$	7	$7\frac{1}{8}$	$7\frac{1}{4}$	$7\frac{3}{8}$	$7\frac{1}{2}$
Continental	53	54	55	56	57	58	59	60	61

SHOES

British and American	3	4	5	6	7	8	9	10
Continental	36	37	38	39	41	42	43	44

STOCKINGS

British and American	8	$8\frac{1}{2}$	9	$9\frac{1}{2}$	10	$10\frac{1}{2}$
Continental	0	1	2	3	4	5

GLOVE sizes are the same in every country.

INDEX

153

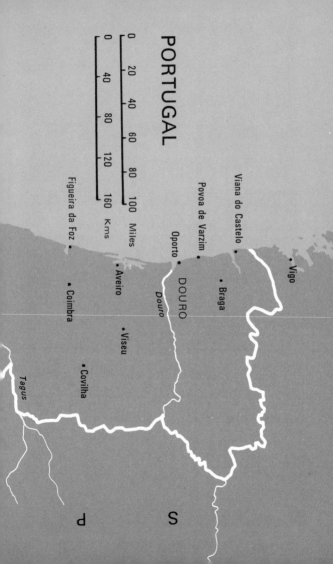

PORTUGAL

| 0 | 20 | 40 | 60 | 80 | 100 | Miles |
| 0 | 40 | 80 | 120 | 160 | Kms |

Viana do Castelo

Povoa de Varzim

Figueira da Foz

Oporto

DOURO

Aveiro

Douro

Braga

Vigo

Coimbra

Viseu

Covilha

Tagus

S

P

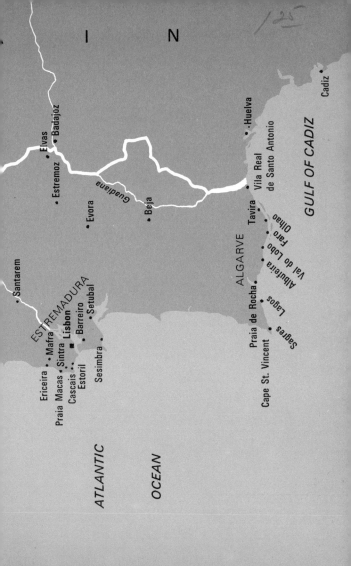